Docker
Essentials

**Simplifying Containerization:
A Beginner's Guide**

MIKE WILSON

© Copyright 2023 - All rights reserved.

The content contained within this book may not be reproduced, duplicated or transmitted without direct written permission from the author or the publisher.

Under no circumstances will any blame or legal responsibility be held against the publisher, or author, for any damages, reparation, or monetary loss due to the information contained within this book, either directly or indirectly.

Legal Notice:

This book is copyright protected. It is only for personal use. You cannot amend, distribute, sell, use, quote or paraphrase any part, or the content within this book, without the consent of the author or publisher.

Disclaimer Notice:

Please note the information contained within this document is for educational and entertainment purposes only. All effort has been executed to present accurate, up to date, reliable, complete information. No warranties of any kind are declared or implied. Readers acknowledge that the author is not engaging in the rendering of legal, financial, medical or professional advice. The content within this book has been derived from various sources. Please consult a licensed professional before attempting any techniques outlined in this book.

By reading this document, the reader agrees that under no circumstances is the author responsible for any losses, direct or indirect, that are incurred as a result of the use of information contained within this document, including, but not limited to, errors, omissions, or inaccuracies.

TABLE OF CONTENTS

INTRODUCTION 1

CHAPTER I: Understanding Docker 3
    What is Docker? 3
    Importance of Containerization in Today's Tech World 6

CHAPTER II: Understanding Containers 10
    Containers vs. Virtual Machines 10
    Benefits of Using Containers 13

CHAPTER III: Setting up Docker 17
    System Requirements 17
    Installation on Different Operating Systems
    (Linux, Windows, MacOS) 20

CHAPTER IV: Docker Architecture 24
    Docker Daemon, Client, and Images 24
    Containers and their Life Cycle 27

CHAPTER V: Docker Commands Basics 31
    docker run, pull, push, build 31
    Inspecting and Managing Containers 34

CHAPTER VI: Docker Images 38
Understanding Image Layers 38
Building Custom Images with Dockerfile 42
Managing Images 45

CHAPTER VII: Docker Networks 50
Network Types: Bridge, Host, Overlay, None 50
Connecting Containers 54

CHAPTER VIII: Docker Volumes and Storage 58
Volume Types and their Usage 58
Bind Mounts and tmpfs Mounts 61
Data Persistence 65

CHAPTER IX: Docker Compose 69
Simplifying Multi-container Applications 69
Writing and Using docker-compose.yml 73

CHAPTER X: Best Practices in Docker 77
Image Optimization 77
Security Best Practices 80
Monitoring and Logging 84

CHAPTER XI: Popular Use Cases of Docker 88
Setting up Development Environments 88
Continuous Integration/Continuous Deployment (CI/CD) 91
Microservices Architecture 95

CHAPTER XII: Docker Ecosystem 100
Docker Hub and Docker Store 100
Introduction to Kubernetes 104

CHAPTER XIII: Troubleshooting Common Docker Issues 108
    Dealing with Container Errors 108
    Network and Volume-related Issues 112
    Resources and Monitoring 115

CHAPTER XIV: Looking Forward- The Future of Docker and Containerization 120
    Ongoing Developments in the Docker World 120
    Emerging Trends 124

CONCLUSION 131
    Docker CLI Reference Guide 131
    Summary 134
    Call to Action 138
    What to look out for in the future 141

INTRODUCTION

The requirement for efficiency, agility, and scalability in software development and deployment has never been higher in an era where technology is developing at a rate never seen before. We are introducing Docker, a revolutionary technology that has completely changed the software containerization market. However, what is Docker exactly? And why has the tech community given it so much praise?

The goal of "Docker Essentials: Simplifying Containerization - A Beginner's Guide" is to serve as your all-inclusive introduction to Docker. Whether you're a computer enthusiast, an IT expert, or an aspiring developer, this e-book tries to provide clear, step-by-step insights into the practical applications of Docker while also demystifying its concepts.

Throughout this guide, you will learn about Docker's architecture, explore its fundamental features, and become comfortable with its command-line operations. We'll explore the intricacies of Docker images, explore the development and maintenance of containers, and dissect the networks and storage systems that make up the Docker ecosystem.

Beyond the fundamentals, we'll cover more complex subjects like Docker Compose, security and optimization best practices, and some of the most well-liked applications where Docker excels. You will have a comprehensive understanding of Docker's capabilities by the end of this e-book and know how to use its power for your projects.

Welcome to Docker's fascinating world. Together, let's take this insightful journey and make the world of containerization easier!

CHAPTER I

Understanding Docker

What is Docker?

In the ever-evolving world of software development, a common challenge that developers and organizations face is environmental inconsistency. This problem often manifests in the infamous "it works on my machine" dilemma, where an application behaves differently across multiple environments. Docker, a revolutionary technology in software containerization, seeks to mitigate this issue by offering a consistent environment for applications to run. But what exactly is Docker, and why has it become a cornerstone in modern DevOps practices?

An open-source platform called Docker was created to simplify the process of building, distributing, and executing applications that use containers. A container can be considered a lightweight, stand-alone, and executable software package containing everything needed to run a code: the application itself, libraries, dependencies, environment settings, and even the operating system. Docker assures that an application will function the same everywhere the container is deployed by combining these components into a package. This level of consistency simplifies the workflow for developers and system administrators alike, ultimately accelerating the software delivery process.

The inception of Docker in 2013 marked a paradigm shift in how we think about software architecture and deployment. Before Docker, Virtual Machines (VMs) were the go-to solution for isolating applications and their environments. While VMs did a decent job ensuring consistency across different platforms, they came with a performance overhead. Each VM runs not just the application but also an entire operating system, which results in slower boot-up times and resource-heavy operation. On the other hand, Docker containers share the host system's OS kernel, eliminating the need for an operating system inside the container. This makes containers incredibly lightweight and fast compared to VMs.

The architecture of Docker is worth mentioning as it comprises several vital components that work in harmony to offer the functionalities it is renowned for. At the core of Docker's architecture is the Docker Engine, a client-server application with three primary components: a server, which is a type of long-running program known as a daemon process; a REST API that indicates interfaces for interacting with the daemon; and a command-line interface (CLI) client. Users interact with Docker through CLI commands or via direct API calls. Furthermore, Docker uses a daemon-client model where the Docker client communicates with the Docker daemon to build, ship, and run Docker containers. The Docker daemon can also communicate with other Docker daemons, opening avenues for container orchestration.

Docker's true power shines when it comes to Docker Images and Dockerfiles. A Docker Image is a lightweight snapshot of a container, acting as a template to produce containers. These images are built from a series of instructions in a text document called a Dockerfile. Once an image is created, it can be shared via Docker Hub, a cloud-based registry service where you can distribute and access Docker images. Organizations and individual developers can quickly pull these images from Docker Hub to create consistent environments.

Another remarkable feature is Docker Compose, a tool for defining and running multi-container Docker applications. With a simple YAML file, you can configure the services, networks, and volumes needed for an application and then bring it all up in a single command ('docker-compose up'). This eliminates the need to manually start each component of an application and link them together, thus making the entire process more efficient and error-free.

Security is also a crucial concern when deploying applications, and Docker addresses this by providing robust isolation capabilities. Containers are isolated from each other and the host system, ensuring they do not interfere. Docker also offers various features like secrets management to handle sensitive information and signed images to verify the authenticity of images, adding an extra layer of security.

One of the reasons Docker has seen such rapid adoption is its wide range of applications. From simplifying local development to being an integral part of continuous integration and continuous deployment, also known as CI/CD pipelines, Docker has diverse use cases. It has gained popularity in the microservices architecture, where each service runs in its container, allowing for better scalability, easier debugging, and more straightforward maintenance. Many companies have even started adopting Docker for machine learning, data analytics, and other data-intensive tasks, proving its versatility.

In conclusion, Docker is more than just a buzzword in today's tech landscape; it is a revolutionary technology that has fundamentally changed how we develop, deploy, and think about software applications. Docker has given software developers a solution to the "it works on my machine" problem and offered a plethora of capabilities that increase the efficiency, security, and flexibility of software development by giving applications a consistent environment to execute in. Whether you are an individual developer or part of a large organization, Docker offers tools that can significantly enhance your software development lifecycle, making it a must-learn technology for anyone in the software industry.

Importance of Containerization in Today's Tech World

In the current landscape of technology, the relentless quest for efficiency, speed, and scalability has become the north star guiding enterprises and developers. At the intersection of this pursuit lies containerization, an innovation that has irrevocably shifted the paradigm of software deployment and application management. So, what makes containerization an indispensable element in today's tech world? To answer this, we must delve into its features, impact on the software lifecycle, and how it synergizes with other tech trends to create a more streamlined and robust ecosystem.

At its core, containerization encapsulates an application and its dependencies in a 'container.' This approach ensures that the application operates consistently across various computing environments. The concept is not entirely new; it draws from older technologies like hardware virtualization and features inherent in operating systems. However, the real magic happened when these concepts were simplified and standardized, most notably by Docker, making it accessible to the masses. Now, developers can easily package an application and its environment into a single container, eliminating the classic "it works on my machine" issue that has plagued the industry for years.

The efficiency gains from using containers are enormous. Traditionally, deploying applications required a whole set of dedicated resources and complicated configurations, often leading to resource wastage and operational overhead. Containers, however, are lightweight by design, utilizing the host operating system's resources to run multiple containers simultaneously without the overhead of running separate OS instances for each application. This efficient utilization of system resources makes it easier to achieve high-density deployments, thereby driving down infrastructure costs.

Speed is another essential attribute that containerization brings to the table. In a world where time-to-market can significantly affect a product's success, the speed at which applications are developed, tested, and deployed is crucial. Containers enable DevOps practices by fostering continuous integration and continuous deployment (CI/CD). In CI/CD pipelines, using containers ensures that the software being developed is always in a deployable state. It allows developers to integrate changes to the codebase frequently, ensuring faster delivery and reducing the time needed to rectify bugs and add features. Containers also allow for quick boot-up times, meaning applications become responsive faster, enhancing user experience and productivity.

Scalability and flexibility, too, are inherent virtues of containerization. Modern-day applications often need to handle varying loads dynamically. Containers can effortlessly scale up or down as per the demand, and orchestrators like Kubernetes can automate this process. Such capabilities are invaluable in microservices architectures, where different services may experience different loads and need to be scaled independently. Also, the portable nature of containers means that they can run anywhere—in on-premises data centers, in the cloud, or even on a developer's local machine—without any modification, providing unprecedented flexibility in deployment options.

Containerization has also revolutionized the way security is handled in application deployment. Isolating applications in containers ensures that they are shielded from each other, reducing the risk of system-wide failures due to a security vulnerability in a single application. Additionally, containerized environments can be scanned for vulnerabilities during the development phase itself, allowing for a more proactive approach to security. Given the growing concerns about cyber threats, this layer of security is no longer optional but a necessity.

However, the significance of containerization isn't limited to isolated use cases; it acts as a catalyst when combined with other technological trends like cloud computing, edge computing, and serverless architectures. For example, many cloud providers now offer container orchestration services that integrate seamlessly with their existing cloud infrastructure, allowing organizations to leverage cloud computing and containerization for maximum efficiency. On the edge computing front, containers enable lightweight, efficient, and consistent application deployments on edge devices, further extending their versatility.

In conclusion, the importance of containerization in today's tech world can hardly be overstated. Its impact on efficiency, speed, scalability, and security has made it a cornerstone in modern software development and operations. Its inherent compatibility with other cutting-edge technologies amplifies its importance, making it a key enabler of current and future tech ecosystems. As organizations increasingly adopt containerization, it's clear that its role is not just that of a facilitator but of a game-changer, setting new standards and practices that will guide the tech world in the future.

CHAPTER II

Understanding Containers

Containers vs. Virtual Machines

In the vast computing universe, two celestial bodies have emerged as dominant forces shaping the landscape of application deployment and system architecture: Containers and Virtual Machines (VMs). Both have revolutionized how applications are developed, deployed, and scaled. However, they offer fundamentally different approaches, advantages, and challenges. To appreciate the nuances between them and understand their unique contributions to modern technology, one must dive deep into their characteristics and explore the implications of each.

Virtual Machines are an abstraction of tangible hardware that can turn a single server into several servers. The concept behind virtual machines dates back decades. Imagine a physical server; an operating system runs atop this, often termed the 'host' OS. A hypervisor, like VMware or Microsoft Hyper-V, operates atop this layer. The hypervisor's responsibility is to create, run, and manage multiple VMs. Each VM, in essence, is a complete system, replete with its own operating system, called the 'guest' OS, along with its libraries, binaries, and the application itself. It's like housing multiple computers within a single physical machine, each with its entire environment.

Containers are a relatively newer phenomenon, mainly popularized by Docker in recent years. They encapsulate the application and its dependencies into a single, isolated unit. Unlike VMs, containers share the same OS kernel as the host but maintain their file systems, binaries, and libraries. This architecture eliminates the need for a guest OS, significantly reducing the overhead. Consider containers as lightweight compartments within an operating system, each tailored for a specific application.

The most apparent distinction between VMs and containers arises from their architectural differences. VMs are heavyweight entities, each carrying the burden of a full OS stack, which can be several gigabytes in size. This leads to significant resource consumption in terms of storage and memory. Containers, devoid of individual OS stacks, are nimble, often only tens of megabytes in size, enabling quicker start-up times and more efficient resource utilization. This size discrepancy also impacts scalability; while a host might run a few VMs, it can quickly run dozens or even hundreds of containers.

Performance is another area where the dichotomy between VMs and containers becomes evident. VMs, given their comprehensive structure, tend to exhibit slower boot-up times. This is especially noticeable in environments requiring rapid scaling or frequent restarts. Containers can start almost instantly by their lightweight design, providing a more responsive environment, especially beneficial in dynamic load situations or microservices architectures.

However, it's not all sunshine and roses for containers. When it comes to isolation, VMs have an edge. Since each VM runs its isolated OS, they offer robust separation, making breaches or failures in one VM unlikely to affect another. While containers provide isolation at the process level, the shared OS kernel poses a vulnerability. All containers on that host could be compromised if a malicious party manages to obtain access to the kernel.

From a management perspective, VMs, having been around longer, enjoy mature tooling, established workflows, and comprehensive support from vendors. Many organizations have substantial investments in VM infrastructure, tools, and expertise. Containers, although they have seen rapid development and growing community support, especially with orchestration tools like Kubernetes, are still in a phase of evolution. Organizations adopting containers face challenges in finding expertise, integrating with existing systems, or navigating the swiftly changing landscape of container technology.

Yet, it's essential to understand that containers and VMs are not mutually exclusive. In many modern architectures, they coexist and complement each other. VMs can provide a robust, isolated environment, housing containers that bring efficiency, speed, and application-centric management. For instance, a cloud provider might use VMs to allocate resources to different clients, with each client deploying their applications in containers within their VMs.

In conclusion, the debate between containers and Virtual Machines is not a zero-sum game. Each offers unique advantages tailored to specific use cases. VMs, with their robust isolation and mature tooling, are apt for scenarios requiring strong separation, legacy application support, or established workflows. With their efficiency, speed, and application-centric design, containers shine in environments emphasizing scalability, performance, and developer agility. As technology advances, the synergy between containers and VMs will likely deepen, resulting in architectures that harness the best of both worlds. The choice is not about picking one over the other, but understanding their strengths and leveraging them in harmony to build robust, efficient, and scalable systems.

Benefits of Using Containers

Containers have become a revolutionary force in the ever-changing world of software development and deployment, providing a solution to long-standing problems and catalyzing the emergence of novel application delivery methods. Containers, encapsulated environments that package an application and its dependencies, have fundamentally altered how developers conceive, build, and deploy software. Delving into the multitude of benefits containers confer will provide a holistic understanding of their rapid ascendancy in the tech world.

At the heart of the container revolution lies the promise of consistency. The perennial challenge "it works on my machine" encapsulates developers' frustrations when code operates seamlessly in one environment but malfunctions in another. Containers assuage this issue. Packaging the application with its dependencies, configurations, libraries, and binaries ensures that the software runs identically regardless of where the container is deployed. This consistent environment bridges the gap between development and operations, streamlining the workflow and obviating discrepancies that often arise between different software lifecycle stages.

Regarding resource utilization and speed, efficiency stands out as another cardinal advantage of containers. Traditional deployment methods, particularly those involving virtual machines, carry the overhead of running multiple OS instances. Containers, however, run on a shared OS kernel, preceding the need for replicating the OS layer. This reduces the container's size, making them lightweight and nimble, and optimizes memory usage and CPU allocation. Consequently, a single server can host a substantially higher number of containers than virtual machines. The slim nature of containers also facilitates rapid start-up, enhancing responsiveness, and ensuring that applications become available to end-users with minimal latency.

Scalability and flexibility, integral for modern applications contending with varying user loads, are inherent to containerized environments. Containers can be swiftly replicated, scaled up or down, or migrated across systems. Orchestrators, like Kubernetes, amplify this benefit by automating containerized applications' deployment, scaling, and management. Containers provide an ideal solution for architectures, especially microservices, where services might require independent scaling based on demand. Their stateless nature and lightweight footprint make horizontal scaling — adding more instances instead of adding more power to a single instance — a seamless endeavor.

Another notable advantage of containers is their contribution to DevOps and Continuous Integration/Continuous Deployment (CI/CD) pipelines. Containers promote an immutable infrastructure where applications are replaced rather than updated, ensuring that the production environment remains consistent and predictable. This is particularly conducive to CI/CD practices, allowing for frequent and reliable software releases. Developers can swiftly integrate changes, test them in a containerized environment identical to production, and ensure that software is always in a deployable state. This agility accelerates software delivery, reduces bug-fixing time, and fosters a culture of collaboration between development and operations teams.

Security, often a prime concern, gains a new dimension with containers. While containers share an OS kernel, they run in isolated user spaces. This means applications within containers are segregated from each other, preventing system-wide failures if a security issue arises in one application. Moreover, given their ephemeral nature, containers can be quickly replaced with updated, secure versions, enabling a proactive response to vulnerabilities. It's worth noting, however, that containers are not a silver bullet for security. Their shared kernel poses potential risks, necessitating vigilance and best practices to ensure a secure containerized environment.

Finally, the portability of containers deserves mention. The "build once, run anywhere" ethos of containers ensures that developers are no longer tethered to specific infrastructure or cloud providers. Whether it's a developer's local machine, an on-premises data center, or a public cloud, containers can operate without modification. This portability alleviates vendor lock-in concerns and allows organizations to choose deployment environments based on cost, performance, or strategic considerations.

In conclusion, containers have ushered in a paradigm shift in software development and deployment. Their myriad benefits, spanning consistency, efficiency, scalability, agility, security, and portability, resonate with the pressing demands of today's digital ecosystem. As organizations strive for faster delivery, streamlined operations, and adaptive systems, containers stand out as both a strategic tool and a transformative agent. Their continued evolution, combined with the burgeoning ecosystem of tools and practices around them, portends a future where software is more resilient, responsive, and aligned with the dynamic needs of businesses and users alike.

CHAPTER III

Setting up Docker

System Requirements

In software development and deployment, Docker stands as a beacon of innovation, offering the allure of containerization - a technique allowing applications to run in an isolated yet consistent environment. Like any robust software tool, Docker has specific system prerequisites that ensure its smooth operation. Understanding these requirements is imperative for anyone seeking to harness Docker's capabilities to its fullest potential.

Docker is a platform designed to enable applications to be created, deployed, and run using containers. As containers package applications and their dependencies into a standardized unit, they guarantee consistent execution across various computing environments. However, to achieve this consistency, Docker has to rely on specific operating system features, thereby defining its system requirements.

Its reliance on the Linux kernel lies at the heart of Docker's architecture. Originally, Docker was developed for Linux, leveraging kernel features like namespaces for process isolation and cgroups for resource management. This underpinning means that any system aiming to run Docker natively would require a Linux kernel. However, the good news is, that Docker's popularity led to its adaptation for non-Linux platforms, like Windows and macOS, albeit with a twist. On these systems, Docker operates by spinning up a lightweight Linux virtual machine behind the scenes, which runs the Docker daemon. It cleverly offers a native feel while harnessing a Linux VM to do the heavy lifting.

Diving deeper, the version of the Linux kernel becomes pivotal. Docker mandates a minimum kernel version, typically 3.10 or higher, to ensure it can leverage all requisite features without glitches. Moreover, the kernel should have support for specific storage and networking drivers to ensure seamless container operation. For example, overlay or overlay2 storage drivers, which manage how container images are stored and organized, are crucial for Docker's efficient functioning.

Equally paramount is the CPU architecture. While Docker runs comfortably on standard x86 architectures, it has seen extensions to others like ARM. This expansion is a testament to Docker's growing ubiquity, finding applications in data centers, edge devices, and IoT setups. Therefore, while x86 remains predominant, Docker's system requirements span a gamut of CPU architectures, catering to diverse use cases.

For those eyeing Docker on Windows, the story takes an exciting turn. Docker Desktop, the iteration for Windows, demands Windows 10 Pro, Enterprise, or Education editions. This stipulation arises from the need for Hyper-V, Microsoft's virtualization technology, which is only available in these versions. Hyper-V facilitates the creation of the Linux VM that Docker relies upon. Moreover, Docker Desktop leans on Windows Subsystem for Linux 2 (WSL 2) for enhanced performance and compatibility, a feature introduced in recent Windows updates.

Regarding macOS, Docker's iteration, Docker Desktop for Mac, encapsulates a strategy similar to its Windows counterpart. It runs a Linux VM, albeit invisibly, using macOS's native hypervisor framework. The requirements, therefore, tilt towards hardware capabilities and OS versions that support this hypervisor. As of my last update, macOS Yosemite 10.10.3 or newer versions are recommended, with hardware support for memory virtualization to ensure smooth sailing.

Another dimension of system requirements is hardware. Irrespective of the platform, running containers necessitates adequate computational resources. While Docker itself has modest needs, the applications running within containers can range from lightweight microservices to heavy databases or data processing engines. A minimum of 4GB RAM is commonly recommended for Docker, with the caveat that the containerized applications would dictate real requirements. Disk space, too, plays a crucial role, especially when dealing with multiple container images, which can often span gigabytes.

Finally, it's worth noting the importance of software prerequisites. Docker's functioning can be influenced by other software components present in the system. For instance, a Docker installation on Linux systems would require a package manager like apt for Ubuntu or yum for CentOS. Furthermore, certain Docker versions might depend on specific library versions or ancillary tools. Staying informed about these through official Docker documentation can prevent potential roadblocks during installation.

In conclusion, Docker, while offering a transformative approach to software deployment, comes with its set of system requisites. These requirements, spanning OS versions, kernel features, CPU architectures, and hardware specifications, are foundational to Docker's promise of consistency and isolation. As Docker continues its march towards ubiquity, evolving to cater to diverse platforms and use cases, staying attuned to these prerequisites ensures that users can harness Docker's power efficiently and without hiccups. It underscores the adage that while innovation often paves the way for simplicity in application, the underlying mechanics often rest on a bedrock of intricate details and requirements.

Installation on Different Operating Systems (Linux, Windows, MacOS)

The appeal of Docker, a tool offering consistent application deployment through containerization, extends across the spectrum of operating systems prevalent today. Its capacity to harmonize the development and deployment environments ensures that irrespective of the OS developers or system administrators use, Docker can be incorporated into their workflow. Installing Docker, however, varies across Linux, Windows, and MacOS, and comprehending these nuances is crucial for a seamless setup.

Beginning with Linux, the birthplace of Docker, the installation process is deeply integrated with the native package management systems. For distributions like Ubuntu, the APT package manager becomes the gateway to Docker. To install Docker on such systems, users often update their local package cache and then retrieve the Docker package. It's worth noting that Docker's official repositories should be used instead of the default OS repositories to ensure the latest, most secure version. Once the repository is set up, the actual installation is as straightforward as installing any other package. However, specific considerations come into play, for instance, allowing the Docker service to start on boot and ensuring the user has permission to access the Docker daemon. Additionally, the versatility of Linux distributions, from CentOS to Fedora and Debian, mandates distinct installation steps tailored to each distribution's unique package manager and system configuration.

Transitioning to Windows, the narrative becomes more intricate. Docker's implementation on Windows is realized through Docker Desktop, a specialized version tailored for the Windows environment. The prerequisite for Docker Desktop is the presence of Windows 10 Pro, Enterprise, or Education, primarily because of the Hyper-V virtualization technology exclusive to these editions. Upon downloading the Docker Desktop installer, the installation is largely guided, with users prompted through a series of steps, including enabling Hyper-V and configuring resources such as CPU and memory. An intriguing facet of Docker on Windows is its duality:

users can switch between Linux and Windows containers. While the former is more prevalent and operates using a lightweight Linux VM in the background, the latter allows native Windows applications to be containerized. Additionally, with the advent of Windows Subsystem for Linux 2 (WSL 2), Docker has further optimized its performance and compatibility, making the integration between Docker and Windows more fluid than ever.

MacOS, with its Unix underpinnings, offers a different landscape for Docker installation. Docker Desktop for Mac leverages the macOS hypervisor framework, HyperKit, obviating the need for additional virtualization software. The installation process is reminiscent of many Mac applications. Users download a '.dmg' file from Docker's official site, and the subsequent steps involve dragging the Docker.app into the Applications folder. Once launched, Docker runs as a native application with a status menu in the macOS menu bar, providing at-a-glance information and controls. Docker on macOS, similar to its Windows counterpart, encapsulates a Linux VM, albeit invisibly to the user. This approach ensures that Docker containers retain their Linux roots, guaranteeing consistency across different deployment environments. As with Windows, resources like memory and CPU cores can be allocated to Docker through its preferences, ensuring that the containers have adequate resources while maintaining system performance.

Despite these OS-specific installation processes, a universal aspect is post-installation verification. After installing Docker, it's common practice to run a sample container, often the 'hello-world' image, to confirm that Docker is installed and operational. This step assures users that their installation was successful and they can proceed to more complex container operations.

In conclusion, Docker's promise of consistent application deployment and execution is upheld across various operating systems. While its roots in Linux make it a native citizen of the Linux world, the adaptations for Windows and MacOS, achieved through virtualization and system-level integrations, ensure that Docker is accessible to most developers and system administrators. The installation processes, tailored to the intricacies of each OS, might differ in their steps and prerequisites, but they converge on the singular goal: providing a robust, efficient, and consistent containerization platform. As Docker continues its trajectory in the tech world, its cross-platform availability underlines its commitment to democratizing container technology, ensuring that irrespective of one's OS allegiance, the benefits of containerization are but a few installation steps away.

CHAPTER IV

Docker Architecture

Docker Daemon, Client, and Images

In the bustling world of containerization, Docker emerges as a linchpin, bridging the divide between software development and deployment. As one delves deeper into Docker's architecture, three components stand out in their importance and function: the Docker Daemon, Client, and Images. Understanding these pivotal components is similar to unraveling Docker's essence, clarifying how Docker achieves its promise of consistent and isolated application environments.

The Docker Daemon, often called 'dockerd', acts as a persistent background process and can be considered the heart of the Docker platform. Operating on a host machine, the daemon is responsible for building, distributing, and running Docker containers. Moreover, it manages Docker objects like networks and volumes, ensuring the ecosystem is interconnected and functional. But its responsibilities don't end there; the daemon listens for Docker API requests, which can come from various sources, including the Docker client, and processes them. This capability allows the daemon to communicate with other Docker daemons, facilitating tasks like image distribution across nodes or hosts. The presence of the Docker Daemon on a machine is a testament to the machine's readiness to engage in Docker operations, be it running a container or managing Docker images.

Adjacent to the daemon, both in terms of function and significance, is the Docker Client. Recognized by the command 'docker,' the client is the primary avenue through which users - be it developers, system administrators, or automation tools - interact with Docker. Every 'docker' command a user types into the terminal is translated into an API call, which is then forwarded to the Docker daemon for processing. The beauty of this client-daemon architecture lies in its flexibility. While they can reside on the same host, facilitating local Docker operations, the client can also communicate with a daemon on a remote machine. This separation allows for versatile setups, such as managing Docker on a cloud server from a local laptop. It's a testament to Docker's distributed ethos, ensuring that control and management are always at one's fingertips, irrespective of where the Docker resources reside.

While the daemon and client facilitate Docker operations, Docker Images are the blueprints that actualize containerized applications. An image is a lightweight, standalone, executable software package encompassing everything needed to run a piece of software, including the code, runtime, system tools, libraries, and settings. Images are immutable, meaning once created, they remain unchanged. This characteristic ensures that an application will run the same, irrespective of where the Docker image is deployed. When a Docker image is run, it metamorphoses into a container, the live and running instance of the image. It's worth noting that while containers are ephemeral, often spun up and destroyed as needed, images are persistent, acting as the repository of application logic and dependencies.

A significant feature of Docker images is their layering mechanism. An image is often built on top of base images, with layers representing file differences. Each instruction in a Dockerfile, the script that dictates how an image should be constructed, creates a new layer in the image. This approach has several benefits. For one, it promotes reusability. Common base images can be shared across multiple projects, ensuring a consistent foundation underpins various applications. Secondly, it optimizes storage. Since layers are shared across images, any change in one layer is stored once, preventing redundancy and conserving disk space.

The Docker Hub, a cloud-based registry, further amplifies the utility of Docker images. It acts as a vast repository where users can push their custom images or pull publicly available ones. Popular software, from web servers like Nginx to databases like PostgreSQL, have official images on Docker Hub, optimized and maintained by the software's creators. This accessibility ensures that setting up complex software stacks becomes a matter of pulling and running the right images, a process that can be accomplished in minutes.

Piecing it all together, one can visualize a typical Docker operation: A user, through the Docker client, issues a command to run a specific image. The client translates this command into an API call, which the Docker daemon receives. The daemon, then, either pulls the image from a registry like Docker Hub or retrieves it from its local cache. Once the image is available, the daemon instantiates it, creating a running container. This containerized application now exists in an isolated environment, defined by the image, ensuring consistent behavior across different hosts or stages of development.

In conclusion, Docker's transformative impact on software development and deployment can be attributed to its intricate yet harmonious architecture. The Docker Daemon, Client, and Images are the triumvirate pillars supporting Docker's containerization paradigm. While the daemon and client facilitate and manage operations, images act as the blueprint, encapsulating applications in their entirety. As Docker continues its ascendancy in the tech world, its architecture, built on the synergy between these components, is a testament to the platform's robustness, flexibility, and efficiency.

Containers and their Life Cycle

In the contemporary tech landscape, containers have become synonymous with efficiency, consistency, and portability in software development and deployment. At the heart of containerization lies the container itself, a technology that encapsulates an application and its dependencies into a consistent environment. As with any technological entity, containers possess a life cycle that elucidates their inception, operation, and eventual termination. Delving into this life cycle offers profound insights into the robustness and versatility of container technology.

Containers find their origins in the desire to isolate applications from the underlying system and each other. At the fundamental level, a container is an isolated user-space instance that runs an application and its dependencies. Unlike traditional virtualization, where each application requires a separate OS instance, containers share the same OS kernel and isolate the application processes from each other. This shared architecture minimizes overhead and accelerates startup times, making containers exceptionally lightweight and fast.

The birth of a container commences with the creation of an image. This image, often crafted using a Dockerfile or a similar script in other containerization tools, contains the blueprint of the application, encompassing the code, runtime, system tools, libraries, and other essential files. Once this image is built, it remains immutable, ensuring the application's consistency wherever the image is deployed. The transition from an image to a live container is akin to the metamorphosis of a blueprint into a tangible entity. When the command to run a container is issued, the containerization tool, such as Docker, takes the image and instantiates it, giving birth to a running container.

Once a container is active, it enters the running phase of its life cycle. It functions like any other application in this state, even within its isolated environment. It can communicate with other containers, the host machine, or external networks, depending on the configurations set during its creation. This ability to function in a networked environment allows containers to form complex applications composed of microservices. Each container can host a specific service, like a database, an API server, or a front-end application, and they can seamlessly interact, creating a cohesive application ecosystem. However, during its running state, a container remains ephemeral. Its existence, in terms of data and state, is transient. If not explicitly stored, any data or state changes within the container will vanish upon its termination.

As with any application, there are moments when a container might need to be paused or stopped. The pausing phase in the container's life cycle allows for temporary halting of the container's processes without terminating it. This can be particularly useful for diagnostic purposes or to temporarily free up system resources. On the other hand, stopping a container halt it and reclaims the system resources, but retains the container's state. This means it can be restarted, returning to its previous running state.

Ultimately, every container reaches the end of its life cycle: the deletion or removal phase. Once a container's task is completed or deemed unnecessary, it can be removed from the system. It's worth noting that removing a container does not delete the underlying image, which remains available for creating new containers. The removal cleans up the resources associated with that particular container instance.

The data persistence challenge is a point of consideration in the container life cycle. Given the transient nature of containers, there's a need to ensure that vital data remains intact beyond a container's life span. Solutions such as Docker volumes or bind mounts come into play here, allowing data to be stored outside the container's file system. This ensures that even if a container is deleted, its associated data remains accessible and can be attached to another container, providing continuity and resilience.

In conclusion, the life cycle of containers represents a harmonious blend of agility, efficiency, and consistency. From their inception as immutable images to their operational phases of running, pausing, stopping, and eventual removal, containers epitomize the modern ethos of software development: rapid, reproducible, and resource-efficient. Their ephemeral nature, while challenging from a data persistence perspective, underscores their role as lightweight, task-specific entities. Like volumes, solutions to the data challenge further highlight the container ecosystem's adaptability and resilience.

As the tech world continues to evolve, containers stand at the forefront of the revolution, reshaping how applications are developed, deployed, and scaled. By understanding their life cycle, developers and system administrators can harness the full potential of container technology, ensuring that applications are robust, performant, flexible, and adaptive to the ever-changing demands of the digital age.

CHAPTER V

Docker Commands Basics

docker run, pull, push, build

Docker has emerged as the frontrunner in containerization, providing developers and system administrators with tools to develop, deploy, and manage applications seamlessly. A suite of commands, each serving specific purposes, powers Docker's functionality. Four commands — docker run, docker pull, docker push, and docker build — form the foundational pillars, orchestrating the life cycle of Docker containers and images. A deep dive into these commands unveils the magic behind Docker's promise of consistency, portability, and efficiency.

At the onset, the docker run command stands out as the linchpin. The command morphs a static Docker image into a dynamic, running container. When executed, docker run performs a series of actions in quick succession: it looks for the specified image locally, and if not found, fetches it from a remote registry like Docker Hub. Upon retrieving the image, Docker creates a container from it and then initiates the main application process within that container. All this happens almost instantaneously, allowing users to launch isolated applications in seconds. The versatility of docker run is evident in its plethora of options. Whether one needs to map ports, mount volumes for data persistence, set environment variables, or define resource limits, docker run accommodates these needs, ensuring that containers are tailored to specific requirements.

While docker run concerns itself with the instantiation of containers, the trio of docker pull, docker push, and docker build revolves around Docker images, the blueprints for containers. The docker pull command is Docker's mechanism for fetching images from remote registries. Whether one is sourcing a base operating system, like Ubuntu, or a software stack, such as the Node.js runtime, docker pull ensures that these images are downloaded and stored locally, ready for instantiation. The simplicity of this command belies its importance. By standardizing where images are sourced from and ensuring that only verified versions are pulled, Docker reinforces its commitment to consistency and security.

On the flip side of docker pull is the docker push command, which facilitates uploading local Docker images to remote registries. Developers who craft custom images, tailored for specific projects or environments, often need to share these with teammates or deploy them across various environments. docker push makes this possible. After tagging an image with the appropriate registry address, executing docker push uploads the image, making it accessible to anyone with the requisite permissions. This command underscores Docker's distributed ethos and fosters collaboration and sharing within the developer community. Public repositories in Docker Hub teem with images shared by developers worldwide, while private repositories offer teams the ability to securely store proprietary or sensitive images.

Completing the quartet is the docker build command, the architect behind Docker images. Crafting a Docker image necessitates a set of instructions, delineating how the base OS should be configured, which software packages need installation, and how the application should be set up. This set of instructions is encapsulated in a Dockerfile. When invoked, docker build reads the Dockerfile, executing each instruction in sequence. The result is a layered Docker image, with each instruction in the Dockerfile corresponding to a layer in the image. This layered approach has two profound implications. Firstly, it optimizes storage. Since layers are reused across multiple images, any common layer must be stored once. Secondly, it ensures reproducibility. Since each Dockerfile instruction translates to an image layer, the process of building an image from a Dockerfile is deterministic, ensuring that the image remains consistent across builds.

In conclusion, Docker's transformative impact on software development and deployment is anchored in its suite of powerful commands. The dance between docker run, which breathes life into containers, and the triumvirate of docker pull, docker push, and docker build, which orchestrate the life cycle of images, paints a picture of a robust and flexible platform. These commands act as the conduits through which Docker's promise of consistency, portability, and efficiency is realized, ensuring that irrespective of where an application is in its life cycle, Docker provides the tools to manage it seamlessly.

Inspecting and Managing Containers

As the digital landscape continues its rapid evolution, the role of containerization, led predominantly by Docker, takes center stage in revolutionizing software development, deployment, and management. However, as developers embrace the container-first approach, the challenges associated with managing many containers become apparent. Herein lies the significance of inspecting and managing containers—two fundamental tasks ensuring containerized applications' robustness, security, and efficiency.

To appreciate the importance of container inspection, one must first understand the complex, multi-faceted nature of containers. At a glance, a container might seem like a simple encapsulation of an application and its dependencies. Yet, underneath this apparent simplicity lies a web of configurations, network settings, storage mounts, and logs that collectively define the container's state and behavior. Without a mechanism to dive deep and inspect these attributes, managing containers would be akin to sailing uncharted waters without a compass.

Docker, understanding the criticality of transparency and introspection, offers a command, aptly named docker inspect. This tool is the magnifying glass through which users can scrutinize every minute detail about a container or an image. Whether one seeks information about a container's IP address, mounted volumes, environment variables, or running status, docker inspect retrieves a comprehensive JSON output, delineating all these attributes and more. This granularity not only assists developers in debugging container issues but also aids administrators in auditing and ensuring container compliance with organizational standards.

Parallel to the importance of inspection is the necessity of container management. With microservices architectures and cloud-native approaches becoming the norm, it's not uncommon for enterprises to deploy hundreds, if not thousands, of containers. Manually overseeing the life cycle of each container is not just impractical but also fraught with risks. Enter container management—Docker's suite of commands designed to facilitate container creation, running, monitoring, and termination.

At the heart of container management is the docker ps command. Its primary function is to list containers, offering insights into their status. A quick run of this command provides a snapshot of all active containers, their IDs, names, ports, and more. Delving deeper, with the -a flag, one can view both running and stopped containers, thereby gaining a comprehensive overview of the container landscape. For situations requiring a focused view, docker ps allows filtering based on criteria such as status, name, or label, ensuring that users can zero in on specific containers precisely.

Beyond just viewing, Docker equips users with tools to interact with and manipulate containers. The docker start, docker stop, and docker restart trio allow for controlling the lifecycle of containers. Whether it's breathing life into a stopped container, pausing an active one, or rebooting one for configuration changes, these commands ensure that containers are in the desired state. Furthermore, the docker exec command permits users to run commands inside a running container for direct interaction. This proves invaluable for debugging, application monitoring, or administrative tasks like updates.

Yet, as one navigates the world of containers, specific challenges arise, like managing container logs. As ephemeral entities, containers, once terminated, leave little trace behind. However, application logs, crucial for debugging and monitoring, need persistence beyond the container's lifecycle. Docker's docker logs command addresses this by retrieving logs from a container. These logs can then be analyzed, stored, or forwarded to centralized logging solutions, ensuring that the application's operational footprint remains accessible.

While Docker's in-built commands offer a robust foundation for container management, the real-world complexity of container orchestration often necessitates more advanced solutions. This recognition has given birth to orchestration platforms like Kubernetes, which, while outside Docker's native purview, magnify the principles of container inspection and management to cater to large-scale, distributed container deployments.

In conclusion, as the tech realm progressively leans into containerization, the dual aspects of inspecting and managing containers crystallize as pivotal. Docker's suite of commands, from docker inspect that delves into container internals, to management tools like docker ps and docker logs, epitomizes the balance between transparency and control. While powerful in isolation, these tools become truly transformative when viewed as parts of a larger ecosystem, encompassing advanced orchestration solutions and cloud-native principles. As enterprises and developers continue their journey in the containerized world, the tenets of inspection and management remain their guiding stars, ensuring that applications are efficient, portable, transparent, manageable, and resilient.

CHAPTER VI

Docker Images

Understanding Image Layers

In the ever-evolving world of software development, containerization has emerged as a beacon of efficiency, reproducibility, and portability. Docker, leading the charge, has revamped traditional deployment and development paradigms by introducing a unique layered approach to software distribution. Central to Docker's innovative design are "Image Layers." While often transparent to the end user, these layers form the bedrock upon which Docker's prowess is built. Delving into the intricacies of image layers, one uncovers the principles and benefits that make them pivotal to Docker's success.

Image layers represent a foundational shift from conventional monolithic software distribution to a modular, incremental approach. Traditionally, software applications were bundled with every dependency, library, and runtime they required, leading to bulky distributions. Docker's layering system reframed this approach by breaking an image into a series of layers, each encapsulating a distinct set of file changes, dependencies, or application binaries.

This breakdown isn't merely a structural change; it introduces many benefits ranging from storage efficiency to rapid deployment.

The magic behind image layers lies in their immutable and shared nature. Once a layer is created, it cannot be altered. This immutability ensures that every layer serves as a consistent building block. If, for instance, a layer is designed to represent a specific version of a library or a set of environmental configurations, users can be assured that the layer will always maintain that state, fostering reproducibility across deployments. In tandem with immutability is the concept of layer sharing. Multiple Docker images often rely on common foundations, like a base operating system or common dependencies. Instead of duplicating these components across images, Docker allows for sharing layers between them. Shared layers are stored once, drastically reducing storage overhead and ensuring efficient use of resources.

Docker's mechanism for constructing images from layers hinges on a particular file known as the "Dockerfile." The Dockerfile is a script of instructions, with each instruction typically creating a new layer. For example, an instruction to install a software package or copy files into the image would create a new layer encompassing those specific changes. When the docker build command is run, Docker reads the Dockerfile, executing each instruction sequentially. As it processes each instruction, a new layer is created, stacked atop the previous ones. This layering is not just conceptual; physically, each layer is stored separately on the disk, and Docker dynamically overlays these layers to present a unified filesystem to the running container.

The benefits of this layered architecture are manifold. Firstly, it introduces unparalleled storage efficiency. Consider a scenario where multiple applications share the same base operating system and a set of common libraries but differ in their application binaries. With Docker's layered approach, the shared layers—the OS and common libraries—are stored once on the disk, while only the distinct application layers differ. This leads to significant storage savings, especially in environments where dozens or hundreds of containers are run.

Moreover, the layered structure enhances the speed of image distribution. When pulling or pushing an image to a registry like Docker Hub, only the layers that aren't already present in the destination are transferred. This differential transfer means that if only a small application layer has changed, only that specific layer is pushed or pulled, resulting in faster image distribution times. This efficiency becomes particularly pronounced in continuous integration and deployment (CI/CD) pipelines, where slight code changes shouldn't necessitate the complete redistribution of the entire application stack.

Beyond efficiencies in storage and distribution, Docker's image layers bolster security. The principle of immutability implies that once an image layer is crafted, it remains unchanged. This unchangeability means that a verified, secure layer can be reused across multiple images without the risk of tampering or alteration. Additionally, security patches or updates can be implemented by merely replacing a specific layer in the stack, ensuring that vulnerabilities are addressed without revamping the entire image.

However, while the advantages of image layers are evident, they also introduce complexities that developers and administrators must be aware of. The layered design necessitates careful crafting of Dockerfiles to ensure that the most changeable content occupies the upper layers, facilitating efficient updates. Additionally, the shared nature of layers means that a single corrupted or compromised layer can impact multiple images, emphasizing the need for rigorous layer verification and security practices.

Docker's image layers are similar to individual threads, weaving together to craft a robust, efficient, and flexible structure in the grand tapestry of containerization. These layers redefine software storage, distribution, and security with their shared, immutable characteristics. While the end-users—be they developers, system administrators, or enterprises—might primarily interact with containers and images as holistic entities, understanding the underpinnings of image layers is crucial. This understanding demystifies Docker's efficiencies, offers insights into optimizing Dockerfile design, and underscores the security and consistency principles intrinsic to containerized software solutions.

In conclusion, as Docker and containerization continue their ascent in the software realm, the layered architecture remains central to their value proposition. Embracing the layered approach is not merely adopting a technical mechanism but a step towards more efficient, reproducible, and secure software development and deployment paradigms.

Building Custom Images with Dockerfile

As the modern software ecosystem shifts from bulky monolithic applications to lean, modular, and scalable microservices, Docker has emerged as the linchpin, redefining deployment, testing, and development paradigms. Central to Docker's versatility is the capacity to craft custom images tailored to unique application requirements. This powerful and transformative capability rests predominantly on the Dockerfile – a blueprint that orchestrates the construction of bespoke images. Exploring the world of Dockerfiles unravels the intricacies of creating custom images, elucidating how they form the nucleus of Docker's vision for the future of software.

Dockerfile, at its core, is a textual representation of step-by-step instructions to create a Docker image. Imagine an artisan meticulously laying brick upon brick, guided by a detailed blueprint, to construct a tower. The Dockerfile serves a similar purpose in the Docker universe. It specifies the base image, identifies the software prerequisites, outlines the necessary configurations, and details the application code that should be present. When this Dockerfile is processed through the docker build command, the resultant artifact is a ready-to-run Docker image, encapsulating the entire software stack it represents.

The journey of crafting an image begins with choosing a foundation. Every Dockerfile commences with a FROM directive, determining the base image upon which additional layers will be stacked. This choice is pivotal, as it delineates the initial operating environment. It could be a minimalistic Linux distribution like Alpine for lightweight applications or more extensive ones like Ubuntu or CentOS, particularly suited for intricate software stacks. This initial decision shapes the resultant image's size, security posture, and compatibility.

With a foundation in place, the Dockerfile turns its attention to the software environment. Utilizing the RUN instruction, developers instruct Docker to execute commands within the image. This is where software packages are installed, system settings are tweaked, and dependencies are satisfied. Each RUN instruction, crucially, results in the creation of a new layer in the image. Hence, Dockerfile authors often amalgamate multiple related commands, using logical operators, into single RUN directives, ensuring the resultant image remains lean and devoid of extra layers.

Applications rarely exist in isolation. They interact, they communicate, and they serve. To facilitate this, the Dockerfile provides instructions like EXPOSE and VOLUME. While the former intimates which network ports the containerized application will use, the latter delineates storage locations outside the container's immediate filesystem, ensuring data persists beyond the container's lifecycle.

Yet, what renders Dockerfiles truly transformative is their ability to encapsulate the application code itself. Using directives like COPY or ADD, source code, binaries, assets, or any requisite files from the developer's environment are transferred into the image. This inclusion ensures that the resultant Docker image isn't just an environment to run the application; it is the application.

Once all components are in place, the Dockerfile culminates with the CMD or ENTRYPOINT instructions. These define the primary purpose of the container — the application it will run by default upon instantiation. It could be a web server, a database, a computational script, or any executable the image is designed to encapsulate.

The beauty of the Dockerfile, however, doesn't rest solely on its structured syntax or its step-by-step nature. It thrives in its capacity to foster reproducibility. With a Dockerfile in hand, any developer can recreate the exact same Docker image regardless of their local setup. This reproducibility eradicates the age-old problem of "it works on my machine." The Docker image becomes the universal constant, ensuring consistency across development, testing, and production environments.

However, the art of Dockerfile crafting isn't without its challenges. Since each directive, especially the RUN instruction, generates a new layer, Dockerfiles must be meticulously designed to prevent bloated images. A haphazardly constructed Dockerfile could lead to large images that are slow to deploy, transfer, and start. Additionally, security is paramount since Docker images can form the basis of production deployments. Using trusted base images, regularly updating software packages to patch vulnerabilities, and minimizing the footprint by including only necessary components are practices Dockerfile authors must embed in their workflow.

Docker's growth, from a developing containerization tool to an industry standard, can be attributed to numerous factors, but its ability to craft custom images via Dockerfiles stands out prominently. By providing developers with a mechanism to define, in granular detail, the construct of their application environment, Docker has democratized software deployment. The barriers of differing development setups, conflicting library versions, or incompatible operating systems fade, replaced by the uniformity of the Docker image.

In conclusion, as the tapestry of software development grows more complex, tools that introduce consistency and reproducibility become invaluable. Dockerfiles, by offering a systematic, detailed, and replicable approach to image creation, form the cornerstone of this new era. They are more than mere scripts; they are the blueprints of modern software deployment, articulating a vision where applications are free from environmental constraints, enjoying the universality, portability, and efficiency that containerization promises.

Managing Images

The embrace of Docker in modern development workflows represents a technological evolution and a philosophical shift. Docker images assume a central role as we transition from monolithic software designs to the modular and isolated realms of containers. They embody the quintessence of applications, capturing the entire software environment, from the operating system to the minute configurations. However, with the ever-increasing reliance on Docker images, managing them efficiently, securely, and systematically becomes paramount. Delving into the art and science of image management uncovers the methodologies and principles that ensure streamlined operations in Dockerized environments.

Despite their fundamental role, Docker images remain inert and static entities until they are instantiated as running containers. As such, they function as templates, master copies from which containers, the actual running instances, are derived. Given their templated nature, Docker images can be stored, transferred, versioned, and shared. It's in these aspects that the discipline of image management emerges.

The primary interface for interacting with Docker images is the Docker CLI (Command-Line Interface). It offers a suite of commands tailored for various image management tasks. For starters, the docker images command lists all locally available images, providing insights into their names, tags, sizes, and creation dates. This overview serves as the entry point, the starting grid from which detailed image management operations branch out.

One of the foundational tasks in image management is the acquisition of images. While Docker images can be crafted locally using Dockerfiles, a vast repository of pre-built images exists on Docker Hub, a cloud-based registry. Using the docker pull command, developers can fetch images from Docker Hub, or any other configured registry, to their local environments. This command ensures that the most recent version of an image, or a specified version using tags, is obtained, facilitating both the adoption of new software releases and the preservation of legacy environments.

Conversely, once an image is crafted or modified locally, it must often be shared or distributed. Whether it's for collaborative development, staging tests, or production deployments, the docker push command allows developers to upload their custom images to registries, making them accessible to teams, CI/CD pipelines, or deployment orchestrators. However, before this distribution can occur, local images must be tagged appropriately using the docker tag command, ensuring they align with repository naming conventions and versioning schemes.

Yet, image management isn't merely about acquisition and distribution. With continuous development cycles, local environments can quickly become cluttered with outdated or unused images, consuming storage and obfuscating relevant images. Here, the docker rmi command steps in, allowing developers to remove specific images. But caution is advised. Deleting an image that underpins existing containers can disrupt operations. Hence, periodic audits and a keen understanding of image dependencies become essential in maintaining a clean and efficient local Docker setup.

However, the physical aspects of storing, fetching, and removing images represent just one dimension of image management. With Docker's rise in prominence, security considerations have taken center stage. Docker images, especially those sourced from public registries, need rigorous vetting. Vulnerabilities, whether unintentional or maliciously embedded, can compromise entire application stacks. Tools like Docker Security Scanning or third-party solutions like Clair and Anchore offer vulnerability assessments, scanning images for known security issues and providing mitigation recommendations.

In addition to security, version control is a pivotal facet of image management. Like source code relies on tools like Git for versioning, Docker images benefit from systematic versioning schemes. Utilizing tags, developers can denote specific versions of images, delineating between stable releases, beta versions, or development builds. This granularity ensures that deployment environments, whether production or development, can precisely select and utilize the intended image version, avoiding inadvertent rollouts of untested or unstable builds.

Furthermore, while Docker Hub remains the most recognized registry, the need for private, controlled, and in-house registries has grown, especially for enterprises. Solutions like Docker Trusted Registry (DTR) or third-party options like Nexus and Artifactory allow organizations to host their Docker images, ensuring control, privacy, and integration with organizational infrastructure. These private repositories, coupled with role-based access controls, audit trails, and integrated security scanning, elevate image management from a mere developmental task to an enterprise-grade operation.

In the broader vista of containerized development and deployment, the significance of Docker images is undeniable. They encapsulate applications, streamline environments, and foster reproducibility. Yet, their very centrality necessitates robust management practices. From the rudiments of local storage management to the complexities of security assessments and enterprise-scale registry operations, managing Docker images is both an art and a science.

In conclusion, as containerization continues its ascendancy in the technological landscape, proficiency in image management becomes non-negotiable. It's a discipline that marries the technicalities of command-line operations with the strategic vision of secure, efficient, and controlled software deployments. In the age of Docker, understanding and mastering image management isn't just a desirable skill; it's imperative for any organization or individual seeking to harness the full potential of containerized solutions.

CHAPTER VII

Docker Networks

Network Types: Bridge, Host, Overlay, None

In the world of containerization, where isolation, scalability, and efficiency are fundamental, Docker stands tall as a frontrunner, revolutionizing how applications are developed, shipped, and run. However, as individual containers in Docker hold specific portions of software stacks, their intercommunication becomes crucial for orchestrating multi-container applications. This is where Docker networking assumes paramount importance, ensuring containers communicate seamlessly amongst themselves and with external entities. The heart of Docker's networking prowess lies in its diverse network types: Bridge, Host, Overlay, and None. Each offers unique features, benefits, and use cases, underscoring Docker's commitment to flexibility and adaptability.

The Bridge network is the networking mode that Docker uses by default. As the name suggests, a bridge network functions as a link, a virtual switch, allowing containers connected to the same bridge to communicate with one another. A default bridge network named "docker0" is automatically created when Docker is installed.

Whenever a new container is spun up without any explicit network configuration, it gets attached to this default bridge, receiving its IP address from a defined range.

However, the bridge network isn't just about inter-container communication within a single host. It also facilitates communication between containers and the external world. When a container wants to communicate externally, the bridge network translates the container's IP address to the host's IP using a mechanism called Network Address Translation (NAT). This ensures containers can access external resources, albeit via the host's interface.

While the default bridge serves many use cases effectively, Docker also allows creating user-defined bridge networks. These user-defined bridges are more versatile and secure than the default bridge. For instance, containers connected to the same user-defined bridge can effortlessly discover each other by their container name, a feature not available in the default bridge.

The Host network is a more straightforward networking mode, bypassing the network isolation between the container and the Docker host. When a container uses host networking, it shares the entire network namespace of its host. In simpler terms, there's no virtual network for containers running in this mode. Instead, they use the host's network stack directly.

The immediate advantage of the host network is performance. Network operations are faster since there's no intermediary bridge or virtual network. Moreover, there's no NAT required to translate container addresses, simplifying the networking stack. However, this direct access comes with a caveat: port conflicts. Since the container and host share the same network space, any port bound by the container is also bound on the host, making the management of ports critical.

A more robust networking solution became imperative as Docker deployments scaled, spanning multiple hosts, possibly even distributed across different data centers or cloud providers. Enter Overlay networks, Docker's answer to multi-host networking. It allows containers across different Docker hosts to communicate with each other as if they were on the same host.

Under the hood, Overlay networks utilize network drivers that employ VXLAN, a network virtualization technology. This ensures containers across different hosts can communicate securely, with their traffic encapsulated until it reaches its target.

But the true brilliance of Overlay networks shines through when integrated with Docker's orchestration tool, Swarm. When a Swarm cluster is initiated, an Overlay network is created by default, ensuring services deployed in the Swarm can communicate across different nodes effortlessly.

The None network is on the other end of the spectrum from the Overlay network. This mode disables all networking. When a container is attached to a None network, it's provided with a network namespace without configuration. Unless specifically configured, the result is a completely isolated container, with no access to external networks, other containers, or even the host.

The None network serves specific use cases where utmost security is required. For instance, highly sensitive tasks, certain security operations, or particular stages of software testing, where complete network isolation is paramount, can leverage the None network type.

The diversity of Docker's networking options is a testament to its versatility. From single-host setups leveraging the Bridge network for straightforward inter-container communication to large-scale, multi-host deployments employing Overlay networks for intricate orchestrations, Docker caters to many scenarios. At the same time, the Host and None networks address edge cases, ensuring high performance or extreme isolation, respectively.

The importance of networking in the containerized ecosystem cannot be understated. As microservices architectures increase, the need for containers to communicate efficiently, reliably, and securely becomes paramount. With its suite of network types, Docker addresses this need adeptly, ensuring that containers encapsulate individual software components; they aren't isolated islands. Instead, they're nodes in a well-coordinated symphony, orchestrated precisely and facilitated by Docker's networking prowess.

As organizations and developers delve deeper into containerization, understanding the nuances, benefits, and use cases of each of Docker's network types is imperative. It's not just about choosing the right tool for the job, but sculpting the very fabric that binds containers, ensuring data flows, services interlink, and applications deliver their intended value. In the vast ocean of containerization, Docker's networking modes are the navigational compasses, guiding, directing, and ensuring seamless journeys.

Connecting Containers

The advent of containerization has redefined the paradigms of software development and deployment. With Docker leading this revolution, isolating software applications into containers ensures modularity, portability, and scalability. But while this isolation is foundational to the success of containers, it also presents a unique challenge: ensuring containers can communicate and collaborate seamlessly. In a world where microservices and distributed architectures are the norm, connecting containers becomes an operational necessity and an art form that balances isolation with interactivity.

At the heart of connecting containers is the understanding that while each container is an isolated environment, mimicking a full-fledged system, it doesn't operate in a vacuum. Just as cells in an organism communicate through intricate networks, so too do containers, relaying data, invoking services, and sharing resources. This connection is established and maintained through Docker's elaborate networking capabilities, ensuring that containers remain isolated units and participants in a cohesive, orchestrated application.

Docker, by default, facilitates inter-container communication through its built-in bridge network. Every Docker installation initializes this default network, ensuring containers, unless specified otherwise, are automatically connected to it. This bridge network acts as an internal network switch, allowing containers to communicate using their IP addresses. Such communication is localized to the host machine, with containers on the same host being able to "see" and interact with one another. However, while this default bridge offers ease of setup, it does have its limitations, especially in terms of DNS-based service discovery.

Docker introduced user-defined bridge networks to overcome the default bridge's constraints. These are custom, user-specified bridge networks that come with enhanced capabilities. Containers connected to a user-defined bridge can communicate using not just their IP addresses, but also their container names. This is a substantial enhancement, simplifying inter-container interactions and reducing the need for hardcoding IP addresses, which can change every time a container is restarted.

However, as applications scale and span multiple hosts, mere bridge networks, whether default or user-defined, become insufficient. It's in this landscape of distributed applications that Docker's overlay network shines. The overlay network type is explicitly designed for multi-host scenarios, such as those orchestrated by Docker Swarm. It connects multiple Docker daemons, ensuring containers across different hosts can communicate as if they were on a single machine. Achieved through sophisticated VXLAN tunneling, this overlay communication remains secure and efficient, irrespective of the underlying physical network's topology.

While these networks cater to specific scenarios, more explicit connections between containers are sometimes desired. Docker's link feature, though now considered legacy, played a role here. It allowed containers to be explicitly linked, ensuring they could communicate and share environment variables. When linked to a web server container, a database container could seamlessly provide the necessary credentials and endpoints. However, with the introduction of Docker's custom networking capabilities, especially the user-defined bridge, the need for explicit linking has diminished, with the more flexible and powerful networking features superseding it.

Beyond these built-in mechanisms, the container ecosystem has seen a proliferation of third-party tools and solutions, each addressing specific nuances of container connectivity. Tools like Weave, Calico, and Cilium have expanded the horizons of Docker networking, introducing features like network segmentation, security policies, and even service mesh capabilities. They cater to advanced use cases, especially in large-scale, enterprise deployments where network topologies become complex, and fine-grained control over container connectivity is essential.

Yet, while technicalities and tools define the mechanics of connecting containers, there's a philosophical dimension to it as well. Containers herald a shift from monolithic applications to microservices. This isn't merely a change in development or deployment strategies but signifies a more profound transformation in how software is conceived. In this new world, each microservice, encapsulated in a container, plays a unique role. It's like an instrument in an orchestra, producing its distinct sound. But the true magic emerges when they all come together, creating a symphony. Connecting containers, ensuring they communicate harmoniously, is akin to orchestrating this symphony.

In conclusion, the realm of connecting containers is both vast and intricate. While the isolation containers provide is revolutionary, ensuring they can connect, communicate, and collaborate unleashes their true potential. With its innate networking capabilities, Docker provides the foundational tools for this connectivity. Simultaneously, third-party solutions expand and enrich these capabilities, ensuring the diverse needs of modern applications are met. As the software world embraces the containerized future, understanding, mastering, and innovating in the art of connecting containers becomes essential. After all, in the grand tapestry of software applications, each container is a thread, and their interweaving and connections, create vibrant patterns of functionality and value.

CHAPTER VIII

Docker Volumes and Storage

Volume Types and their Usage

In the evolving landscape of containerization, Docker remains at the forefront, changing how applications are developed, deployed, and run. As these containers offer isolated environments for running applications, they're intrinsically ephemeral by nature, meaning their lifecycles are transient. While this temporary nature is a boon for ensuring consistency and reproducibility across environments, it poses a significant challenge regarding data persistence. This is where Docker volumes, with their varied types and usages, come into play, offering solutions to the problem of balancing container ephemerality with the need for persistent data storage.

The essence of Docker volumes lies in their capability to facilitate external storage areas, independent of the container's lifecycle. When a container is deleted, the volume remains untouched, ensuring data remains intact. This ensures that data, whether it's application logs, databases, or configuration files, can transcend the transient nature of containers, providing a continuum in the otherwise ephemeral world of containerization.

To begin with, it's imperative to understand the basic, or as Docker calls it, the 'local' volume. Local volumes are the most straightforward volume type. Created and managed by Docker, they reside on the host's filesystem but are isolated from the core container filesystem. The advantage of this isolation is twofold. First, it ensures data persists beyond the container's life. Second, keeping the volume separate allows data to be shared and reused across containers. The ease of creating local volumes, often with a simple Docker command, has made them a staple in many containerized setups, especially where basic data persistence or sharing between containers on the same host is essential.

However, the need for more advanced volume solutions becomes apparent as Docker deployments grow in complexity, especially in distributed, multi-host environments. Enter volume drivers. These plugins provide the ability to create and manage volumes outside the local host's filesystem. With volume drivers, Docker can interface with external storage platforms, whether cloud-based solutions like Amazon EBS or software-defined storage systems like RexRay. This opens a plethora of possibilities. Suddenly, containers running on different hosts can share data seamlessly. Backup, replication, and scaling of storage become more manageable, leveraging the inherent capabilities of these external storage systems. And all of this while ensuring the volume remains decoupled from any specific container's lifecycle.

Another pivotal concept in Docker's storage strategy is 'bind mounts.' While they might seem similar to volumes on the surface, bind mounts have distinct characteristics and use cases. A bind mount is a process of mounting a specific directory or file from the host into the container. This provides the container direct access to parts of the host's filesystem. It's an approach that's both powerful and dangerous. The power comes from its simplicity and the ability to provide real-time data access between the host and container. The peril, however, lies in this very power. Since containers can read and possibly modify the host's filesystem directly, there's a heightened risk of unintended data alterations or data corruption. Hence, while bind mounts are invaluable in specific scenarios, especially during development phases or when real-time data sharing is a priority, their usage necessitates caution.

Further enriching Docker's storage arsenal is the concept of 'tmpfs mounts.' This is a more transient form of storage, where data is stored only in the host's memory, never touching the physical storage. As a result, tmpfs mounts offer blazing fast read and write capabilities, making them ideal for scenarios where speed trumps persistence, such as caching or temporary data processing. However, their volatility, with data vanishing when a container is stopped or the host is rebooted, limits their use cases to specific scenarios where data persistence isn't a priority.

Understanding these volume types is only half the battle. The true mastery lies in knowing when to use which. Local volumes are the go-to for most standard use cases, offering a blend of simplicity and persistence. With their ability to interface with external storage solutions, volume drivers are pivotal in larger, distributed setups where data sharing across hosts or advanced storage functionalities are necessary. Bind mounts, with their direct link to the host's filesystem, offer unparalleled real-time data sharing but come with risks and are best suited for development environments or specific production scenarios where their benefits outweigh their potential hazards. And tmpfs mounts, with their ephemeral nature, are reserved for those unique situations where speed is of the essence, and data loss is an acceptable trade-off.

In conclusion, in the vast, dynamic realm of Docker and containerization, volumes stand as silent sentinels, guarding the sanctity of data. They bridge the gap between the ephemeral world of containers and the perennial need for data persistence. Each volume type, with its characteristics, advantages, and considerations, offers unique solutions to varied data challenges. As developers and system administrators delve deeper into the world of containerization, understanding these volumes isn't just beneficial; it's imperative. After all, in the intricate dance of containers, while agility and isolation are essential, the persistence and continuity of data provide the rhythm, ensuring the dance remains graceful and grounded.

Bind Mounts and tmpfs Mounts

In the intricate symphony of containerization orchestrated by Docker, a nuanced dance of data exists. Data, in all its myriad forms, represents the living essence of any application. Yet, the ephemeral nature of containers poses an exciting challenge to data persistence and real-time interaction. Navigating this problem requires understanding Docker's diverse storage strategies, two of which stand out for their unique properties: bind mounts and tmpfs mounts.

While different in their operations and use cases, these two strategies exemplify Docker's commitment to providing flexible data solutions for varied needs.

Diving into bind mounts first, we are introduced to one of Docker's most straightforward yet powerful data-sharing mechanisms between the host and the container. At its core, a bind mount is the process of mapping, or 'binding,' a specific directory or even a singular file from the host's file system into the container's file system. This direct mapping means the container can access this data as if it were natively part of its environment.

The implications of such a design are significant. For developers, bind mounts offer a compelling proposition: real-time data interaction. Imagine a scenario where a developer is actively writing code on their local machine, and with every save, the changes are immediately reflected within the container environment. This real-time mirroring, facilitated by bind mounts, transforms development workflows, making them more dynamic and interactive. It eradicates the need for repeatedly rebuilding images or restarting containers every time there's a change in the codebase.

However, as with all things powerful, bind mounts come with their own caveats. The essence of bind mounts, their direct access to the host's file system, can be a double-edged sword. Since containers are designed to be separate units, there should be as little risk to the host as possible. But with bind mounts, this isolation can be somewhat compromised. A misconfigured container, or worse, a malicious one, can inadvertently or intentionally modify or corrupt the host's data.

This risk necessitates a measured approach to bind mounts, ensuring they are used judiciously, with the appropriate read or write permissions.

Transitioning from the directness of bind mounts, tmpfs mounts introduce us to a different data management paradigm. Instead of relying on the physical storage of the host, tmpfs mounts leverage the host's system memory (RAM) to store data. This ephemeral storage strategy creates a temporary file system, residing entirely in memory, which can be mounted into the container.

The allure of tmpfs mounts lies in their blazing speed. With data operations occurring entirely in RAM, read and write actions achieve speeds that traditional disk operations simply cannot match. This makes tmpfs mounts ideal for specific use cases where performance is paramount. Consider, for instance, scenarios requiring high-speed caching or temporary data processing. Here, the transitory nature of the data, combined with the need for swift operations, makes tmpfs mounts the optimal choice.

However, the very strength of tmpfs mounts, their volatility, is also their most significant limitation. Data stored in a tmpfs mount is as ephemeral as it gets. Once the container is stopped, or in the event of a host system reboot, the data vanishes, lost to the ether. While acceptable in scenarios where data loss is not a concern, this transient nature makes tmpfs mounts unsuitable for use cases requiring any form of data persistence.

Both bind mounts and tmpfs mounts, in their distinct ways, underscore Docker's philosophy of flexibility. They cater to specific needs, ensuring developers and system administrators have the right tools for the right job. With their real-time data reflection, bind mounts are transformative for development environments and scenarios where direct interaction between the host and container data is necessary. Their power, however, mandates a responsible approach, ensuring the sanctity and security of the host's data.

On the other hand, tmpfs mounts, with their transient storage strategy, represent the epitome of performance in Docker's data solutions. They cater to those unique use cases where speed is of the essence, and data persistence is secondary. Their use underscores the evolving nature of data strategies in containerized environments, where traditional storage notions are being redefined.

In conclusion, as containerization continues to redefine the contours of software development and deployment, understanding the nuances of data becomes pivotal. Bind mounts and tmpfs mounts with characteristics, advantages, and limitations represent key tools in Docker's data arsenal. They serve as a testament to Docker's commitment to addressing the diverse needs of its vast user base, ensuring that in the world of containers, data, in all its forms and functions, finds its rightful place. Whether it's the direct, real-time interactions of bind mounts or the swift, fleeting operations of tmpfs mounts, Docker offers solutions that balance performance, persistence, and flexibility, crafting a holistic data narrative in the ever-evolving container ecosystem.

Data Persistence

In the vast software deployment and development universe, containerization has emerged as a paradigm-shifting force. Pioneered by platforms like Docker, this approach promises consistency, scalability, and isolation. Yet, amid the myriad advantages of containerization lies a complex challenge: the inherently ephemeral nature of containers. By design, containers are transient, providing isolated and reproducible environments that can be effortlessly spun up and torn down. While ensuring consistency and reducing "it works on my machine" issues, this ephemeral design confronts the perennial requirement of data persistence head-on. How does one maintain the integrity and continuity of data in an environment where everything is designed to be short-lived?

At the heart of Docker's solution to this problem is its robust system for data persistence. Recognizing that applications are more than just stateless processes – that they often require a way to store, retrieve, and maintain state – Docker introduced mechanisms to bridge the gap between the fleeting life of containers and the enduring nature of data. Through volumes, bind mounts, and tmpfs mounts, Docker offers a spectrum of solutions, each tailored to specific needs and scenarios.

In Docker's lexicon, volumes are perhaps the most potent tool for achieving data persistence. While containers come and go, volumes remain steadfast, ensuring that data outlives any specific container instance. When a developer or system administrator initializes a volume, it exists outside the container's filesystem. This decoupling is fundamental. It ensures that even if a container is deleted, the volume – and more importantly, the data within – remains untouched. This persistence mechanism allows for scenarios where multiple containers can be sequentially or simultaneously attached to the same volume, sharing or inheriting data as needed.

However, Docker's commitment to flexibility is evident in its handling of volumes. Recognizing that the storage world is vast and varied, Docker introduced volume drivers. Beyond the default local storage, these drivers allow Docker volumes to interface with popular storage solutions, from cloud offerings like Amazon EBS to network storage systems like NFS. This integration not only amplifies Docker's storage capabilities but also brings to the table advanced features inherent to these storage solutions, such as replication, backup, and remote accessibility.

Bind mounts, another arrow in Docker's data persistence quiver, offer a more direct approach to data storage. By allowing a specific directory or file on the host's filesystem to be 'mounted' directly into the container, bind mounts provide an avenue for real-time data sharing between the host and the container. This is an advantage for developers, especially during the development and testing phases. Code or data changes on the host can be immediately reflected inside the running container, streamlining workflows. Yet, this direct access, while powerful, necessitates caution. If not managed correctly, the porous boundary introduced by bind mounts can lead to unintentional data modifications or even breaches.

For scenarios where speed is paramount and persistence secondary, Docker introduces tmpfs mounts. Unlike volumes or bind mounts that rely on some form of persistent storage, tmpfs mounts utilize the host's RAM, creating an in-memory storage solution. This ephemeral strategy ensures lightning-fast data operations, ideal for caching, temporary data manipulation, or any use case where data doesn't need to survive beyond the container's lifecycle.

Yet, Docker's approach to data persistence is more than just a trio of storage solutions. It's underpinned by a more profound philosophy: recognizing data's central role in the application lifecycle. In this philosophy, data isn't just an afterthought; it's a first-class citizen. Docker's extensive CLI commands related to data management, its integrations with storage platforms, and its continuous enhancements in the data domain underscore its commitment to ensuring that data persistence is as integral to the containerization narrative as the containers themselves.

Furthermore, while technically sound, Docker's data strategies also bear the mark of practicality. They're designed with real-world use cases in mind. Whether it's a developer looking for a streamlined code-test-deploy cycle, a data scientist requiring quick data manipulations without persistence, or an enterprise aiming for robust, long-term storage solutions with failover capabilities, Docker's array of data persistence tools caters to the spectrum.

In conclusion, as containerization continues its ascent as a dominant force in the software world, the challenge of data persistence remains central. With its multifaceted approach, Docker has showcased that data's permanence can be achieved, managed, and optimized even in an environment defined by transience. It serves as a testament to the platform's vision – a vision where containers, in all their transient glory, coexist seamlessly with data, in all its enduring grandeur. In Docker's world, data persistence is not just a technical challenge; it's a harmonious blend of technology, strategy, and vision, all working in tandem to ensure that amidst containers' fleeting lives, the data narrative remains continuous, consistent, and coherent.

CHAPTER IX

Docker Compose

Simplifying Multi-container Applications

Containerization, pioneered by platforms like Docker, has not only transformed the landscape of software deployment but has also ushered in a new era of application development and management. At the heart of this transformation is encapsulation, where every service or component of an application is neatly packed into a container, ensuring reproducibility, scalability, and isolation. However, the real-world complexity of applications often goes beyond a single container. Most contemporary applications are multifaceted, involving multiple services that must interact, share data, and maintain their respective isolated environments. Docker's approach to managing these multi-container applications symbolizes its commitment to simplicity and power, paving the way for an orchestrated dance of containers that function harmoniously while preserving their distinct identities.

The promise of containerization is twofold: while it provides isolated and consistent environments for individual services, it also recognizes the interconnected nature of these services in forming a holistic application. Consider, for instance, a typical web application. It may involve a web server running in one container, a database service in another, and perhaps a caching layer or a background job processing system in others. Each of these services has its unique requirements, configurations, and dependencies. Docker containers provide the perfect encapsulation for such diverse services, ensuring each can run in an environment tailored to its needs. Yet, the magic of the application lies not just in these isolated services but in their orchestrated interactions.

Introducing Docker Compose, Docker's answer to managing multi-container applications. While individual Docker commands are powerful in managing single containers, Docker Compose introduces a higher-level abstraction, allowing developers to define and manage an entire ecosystem of interconnected containers using a single, declarative configuration file. The simplicity of this approach cannot be overstated. Instead of juggling multiple commands and configurations for each service, developers can lay out the entire application topology in a 'docker-compose.yml' file, detailing service configurations, network connections, shared volumes, and more. With a single command, 'docker-compose up,' the entire application springs to life with all its interlinked services.

But Docker Compose's brilliance isn't confined to its simplicity. It's in the granular control it offers over the multi-container environment. Within the 'docker-compose.yml' file, developers can specify the exact version of the image for each service, set environment variables, map ports, define volumes for data persistence, and even determine the startup order of services, ensuring that dependencies are respected. For instance, guaranteeing a database container is fully operational before launching a web server that depends on it.

Beyond local development and testing, Docker Compose also streamlines the transition to production. The same 'docker-compose.yml' file that defines the application on a developer's local machine can be used to deploy the application stack on a production server. This consistent representation of the multi-container application across different environments minimizes the infamous "it works on my machine" problems, ensuring a smooth and predictable deployment process.

Yet, as applications grow and scale, they often transcend the boundaries of single-host deployments. In scenarios involving multiple servers or even entire data centers, Docker extends its orchestration capabilities with platforms like Docker Swarm and integration with Kubernetes. These orchestrators take the principles of multi-container management to a grander scale, handling service discovery, load balancing, scaling, and even self-healing of services. While Docker Compose lays the foundation by defining the multi-container application, orchestrators like Swarm and Kubernetes operationalize this definition in large-scale, distributed environments.

It's essential to understand that the philosophy underpinning Docker's approach to multi-container applications isn't just about managing complexity; it's about transforming it. Docker allows developers to focus on what truly matters: building and deploying great applications by abstracting away the intricacies of service interactions, network configurations, and dependency management. This high-level perspective, where the application's architecture and flow become paramount, and the nitty-gritty of container management fades into the background, is Docker's true gift to the developer community.

However, Docker's orchestration of multi-container applications isn't just a technical marvel; it's emblematic of a broader shift in the software world. As microservices architectures gain prominence, the need for tools that can seamlessly manage and orchestrate numerous interdependent services becomes paramount. With its comprehensive suite of tools and platforms, Docker is at the forefront of this movement, ensuring that as applications fragment into smaller, more focused services, the tools to manage, deploy, and scale them remain holistic, integrated, and, above all, simple.

In conclusion, Docker's approach to simplifying multi-container applications is a testament to its vision of the future of software development and deployment. Recognizing the increasing complexity of modern applications, Docker provides tools that transform this complexity into simplicity, power, and elegance. Whether it's through the declarative nature of Docker Compose, the scalability of Swarm and Kubernetes, or the sheer consistency of containerized environments across the development-production spectrum, Docker ensures that in the world of multi-container applications, simplicity and power go hand in hand. As the software landscape continues to evolve, Docker stands as a beacon, illuminating the path toward a future where multi-container applications are manageable and a joy to develop, deploy, and maintain.

Writing and Using docker-compose.yml

In the panorama of software development and deployment, the rise of containerization has been nothing short of revolutionary. Among the suite of tools that have propelled this revolution, Docker stands out for its robust container management capabilities and foresight in addressing the challenges of orchestrating multi-container applications. One of the most emblematic manifestations of this foresight is Docker Compose and its configuration file: docker-compose.yml. This section delves into the nuances of writing and using this file, shedding light on its transformative impact on how developers conceive, structure, and deploy multi-container applications.

The docker-compose.yml file is the linchpin of Docker Compose, a tool specifically designed to manage and orchestrate multiple Docker containers. At its core, Docker Compose allows developers to define, in a single file, all the services, networks, and volumes that constitute their application, offering a unified view of what might otherwise be a complex web of interconnected containers. The allure of Docker Compose lies in its promise of simplicity: the ability to define an entire application stack in one place, and then, with a few commands, bring it to life or tear it down.

A docker-compose.yml file can seem daunting for those uninitiated, but its structure is rooted in clarity and hierarchy. It starts by defining various services, each representing a container and its configuration.

For instance, in a typical web application, one might have services for a web server, a database, and a caching layer. Each service definition encompasses details like the Docker image to be used, environment variables, ports to be exposed, and networks and volumes to connect to.

However, beyond the mere enumeration of services and their properties, the real prowess of the docker-compose.yml file lies in its ability to express relationships and dependencies between these services. Consider the example of a web server that relies on a database. Within the Compose file, one can specify that the web service should wait for the database service to be fully initialized before starting, elegantly handling startup dependencies. This is achieved through constructs like the depends_on directive, illustrating how the docker-compose.yml file isn't just a static descriptor but a dynamic blueprint of application behavior.

Networking, another cornerstone of multi-container applications, is also elegantly handled in the Compose file. Docker Compose allows developers to define custom networks, effectively dictating how services communicate with each other. By default, all services in a Compose file are part of a single default network, ensuring they can discover and communicate with each other. However developers have the flexibility to create multiple networks, isolating certain services or defining specific communication pathways, offering a granular control over inter-service communication.

Data persistence and management, an integral aspect of many applications, finds its place in the Compose file through volumes.

Developers can define named volumes, ensuring data persists beyond the lifecycle of containers, and then attach these volumes to services, creating shared or dedicated data stores. This aspect of the docker-compose.yml underscores Docker's commitment to treating data with the same first-class status as application code, ensuring that data persistence and portability are as streamlined as application deployment.

Writing the docker-compose.yml file involves a keen understanding of the application's architecture and the relationships between its various components. But once written, the rewards are manifold. With the file in place, commands like docker-compose up become potent, translating the static definitions in the file into a living, breathing application. Moreover, Docker Compose ensures consistency. The same Compose file can be used across development, testing, staging, and production environments, ensuring that the application behaves predictably across various stages of its lifecycle.

But the most profound impact of the docker-compose.yml file is conceptual. It encourages developers to think of their applications not as monolithic entities but as compositions of interlinked services. This mindset dovetails perfectly with the broader industry trend towards microservices – a paradigm where applications are structured as collections of loosely coupled, independently deployable services. By offering a tool that makes managing such multi-service applications straightforward, Docker Compose, and by extension, the docker-compose.yml file, is at the vanguard of this architectural evolution.

In conclusion, the docker-compose.yml file is emblematic of Docker's philosophy: a blend of simplicity and power. Its declarative syntax offers developers a holistic view of their application, capturing not just its components but also their intricate relationships. But it's not just a passive descriptor; coupled with Docker Compose commands, it becomes a dynamic tool, able to instantiate complex applications with a single command. As software architecture continues its march towards modularity and decentralization, tools like Docker Compose, underpinned by the docker-compose.yml file, will be indispensable, guiding developers through the challenges of this new era and ensuring that the promises of containerization are fully realized.

CHAPTER X

Best Practices in Docker

Image Optimization

As the digital world evolves, efficiency and speed have become indispensable tenets of modern software applications. Docker is a prominent tool in the containerization space that enables developers to bundle and distribute applications in a uniform manner. Central to Docker's ecosystem is the concept of images. However, Docker images can range from lean and efficient to bloated and cumbersome like any software artifact. This section aims to shed light on the importance of image optimization in Docker and provides a deep dive into strategies and best practices to achieve efficient, compact, and performant Docker images.

Docker images serve as blueprints for containers. Every image is a packaged version of an application, including all its dependencies, libraries, and binaries. Since containers are meant to be lightweight, it is imperative to ensure that the Docker images they are based on are also lightweight. A streamlined image reduces the storage footprint and results in quicker pull and push times, faster container start-up, and improved overall application performance. Moreover, optimized images also improve security, as they minimize the attack surface by including only the necessary components.

At the heart of Docker's image efficiency lies its layered architecture. Every Dockerfile action— an installation command, copying files, or setting environment variables—creates a new layer. The understanding and prudent management of these layers are pivotal to image optimization. For starters, it is good practice to minimize the number of layers. Combining commands in a Dockerfile, wherever possible, ensures that fewer layers are generated. For instance, chaining installation commands in a single RUN directive instead of multiple lines can make a significant difference.

Additionally, the order of instructions in the Dockerfile plays a critical role. Since Docker uses a caching mechanism for image layers, placing frequently changed instructions toward the end of the Dockerfile can leverage this cache effectively. For example, if an application's source code changes regularly, copying it into the image after installing the application's dependencies is advisable. This ensures the dependency installation layer is cached and reused, while only the source code layer is rebuilt.

Another crucial aspect of optimizing Docker images is being selective about what gets added to the image. It's not uncommon for developers to inadvertently include unnecessary files or tools in their images. Utilizing a .dockerignore file can mitigate this. Similar to a .gitignore file, this file lets developers list files or directories that need to be removed from the image. This can prevent including local configuration files, caches, or unnecessary logs in a production container.

One of the most significant contributors to image bloat is unused software packages or dependencies. During the development phase, various tools or libraries are often installed for debugging or testing. While invaluable during development, these tools have no place in a production image. Regularly auditing the installed packages and removing the redundant ones can drastically reduce image size. Moreover, when installing packages, it's a good practice to avoid installing recommended or suggested packages if they aren't essential.

A strategic approach to base images can also lead to substantial optimizations. Docker Hub, Docker's official image repository, offers many base images. While it might be tempting to opt for full-fledged OS images, a minimalistic image like Alpine Linux can be a better choice in many cases. These lightweight images provide just enough to run most applications but come without the overhead of unnecessary packages or tools, resulting in much smaller final image sizes.

Furthermore, after building an image, tools like docker image prune can remove unused images, freeing up space. Third-party tools and utilities, such as Dive or Slim, can analyze and help reduce Docker image sizes by providing insights into what's consuming space or suggesting optimization strategies.

Beyond size considerations, image optimization also encompasses security. Every additional package or library in an image is a potential vulnerability. By minimizing the components in an image, the attack surface is reduced. Regularly updating the base images and dependencies ensures that any known vulnerabilities are patched. Automated tools, like Clair or Trivy, can scan Docker images for security vulnerabilities and provide recommendations for mitigation.

In conclusion, image optimization in Docker is a multifaceted endeavor that spans size, performance, and security considerations. An optimized image is not just a boon for developers and operators but also crucial for end-users who benefit from faster, more responsive applications. By understanding Docker's layered architecture, being informed about what goes into an image, selecting the right base images, and regularly auditing and updating images, developers can guarantee that their Docker images are not only lightweight and fast but also secure and robust. In a world where microseconds can make a difference and security breaches can have profound implications, Docker image optimization is not just a best practice—it's an imperative.

Security Best Practices

In the ever-evolving landscape of modern software development, Docker has emerged as a cornerstone for many businesses, providing an efficient way to package, ship, and run applications in various environments. With its meteoric rise in popularity, Docker's security has become paramount. As with any technology, vulnerabilities can be exploited, and without diligent attention to security, organizations can inadvertently expose themselves to significant risks. This section delves deep into the realm of Docker security, emphasizing the best practices to ensure that Dockerized applications are functional and secure.

At its core, Docker is about containers—lightweight, standalone, and executable software packages that include everything an application requires to run: code, runtime, system tools, system libraries, and settings. Containers, by being isolated, offer an inherent layer of security. However, the same features that make Docker powerful, such as its ease of use and flexibility, can also introduce security challenges if mismanaged.

One of the foundational principles of Docker security is the concept of least privilege. This principle posits that every process should run with the minimum set of privileges necessary to complete its task, thereby reducing the potential damage of a security breach. In Docker's context, this means containers should be run as non-root users whenever possible. If compromised, a container run as a root user could potentially allow malicious actors to gain root access to the host system, leading to catastrophic consequences.

The choice of base image is another critical consideration in Docker security. Images form the foundation of containers, and a vulnerable image can introduce risks to every container derived from it. It's essential to source images from reputable sources, preferably official images on Docker Hub or trusted vendors. Regularly updating these images ensures they benefit from patches and fixes for known vulnerabilities. Tools like Clair, Anchore, or Trivy can assist in scanning Docker images for known security vulnerabilities, providing an extra layer of assurance.

Network configurations in Docker also merit careful attention. Docker provides various network modes, and while it might be tempting to use the default bridge network for ease, it's often beneficial to customize network settings for enhanced security. For instance, inter-container communication can be disabled unless explicitly required, reducing the potential for lateral movement in case of a breach. Employing user-defined bridges or better yet, Docker's overlay networks, can further enhance container isolation and communication security.

Persistent data storage, a crucial aspect of many applications, is facilitated in Docker through volumes. While volumes are efficient in handling persistent data, they can also be a potential security loophole. To mitigate this, managing volume permissions diligently is essential and ensuring that sensitive data, like secrets or credentials, isn't stored directly in containers or images. Docker has introduced secrets management in Swarm mode, providing a safer way to handle sensitive information.

The Docker daemon, the background service that manages Docker containers, is another potential attack vector. As the Docker daemon requires root privileges, any compromise can be detrimental. To safeguard against this, enabling and configuring Docker's daemon-level security features is advisable. For instance, the Docker daemon can be bound to a Unix socket instead of a TCP port, reducing remote access possibilities. Additionally, using TLS encryption when the

Docker API requires remote access ensures that only authenticated clients can communicate with the Docker daemon.

Monitoring is an often overlooked yet critical component of Docker security. Regularly monitoring container activity can help in detecting anomalous behaviors. Tools like Falco or Sysdig can assist in real-time security monitoring, setting rules and alerts for suspicious container activities. This proactive monitoring is invaluable for detecting potential breaches and understanding regular application behavior, making deviations more noticeable.

Another essential practice in Docker security is ensuring regular updates. Like any software, Docker is continually evolving, with newer versions often including patches for known vulnerabilities. Regularly updating Docker itself and the containers ensures they are safeguarded against known issues. It's also worthwhile to stay updated with Docker's own security documentation and advisories, which often provide insights into best practices and known vulnerabilities.

Docker also offers built-in security features like seccomp profiles, AppArmor, and SELinux, which can be configured to enhance container security. These features provide fine-grained control over container permissions, system calls, and access controls. While they might introduce complexity in setup and management, their benefits in bolstering container security are undeniable.

In conclusion, Docker has revolutionized developers' thinking about, developing, and deploying software. Its advantages in flexibility, scalability, and consistency are irrefutable. However, like any tool, Docker must be used with a discerning eye on security. By adhering to the principles of least privilege, diligently choosing and managing images, carefully configuring networks and volumes, monitoring container activity, and regularly updating Docker and its components, organizations can reap all the benefits Docker offers without compromising security. In a digital world where threats evolve daily, being proactive, informed, and meticulous in security practices is not just advisable—it's necessary.

Monitoring and Logging

In today's complex IT environments, monitoring and logging have become indispensable components of a robust operational strategy. As Docker continues to gain traction as a leading containerization platform, understanding the intricacies of monitoring and logging within Docker environments becomes crucial. These activities help maintain the health and performance of containerized applications and provide critical insights into potential security threats and operational anomalies. This section explores the significance, methodologies, and best practices associated with monitoring and logging in Docker.

Docker has transformed the landscape of software deployment by enabling developers and operations teams to package applications and their dependencies into isolated containers. This isolation ensures consistency across different stages of the application lifecycle. However, the dynamic nature of containerized environments, often characterized by the frequent creation and destruction of containers, introduces unique challenges in monitoring and logging. Unlike traditional monolithic applications, where monitoring a single application instance often sufficed, Docker environments necessitate a more granular approach.

At the heart of Docker monitoring lies the understanding of container health. While it's tempting to view a container as a black box, solely focusing on whether it's running or not, such a simplistic approach can lead to oversight of potential performance bottlenecks or errors. Comprehensive Docker monitoring entails tracking many metrics, including CPU usage, memory consumption, network IO, disk IO, and more. These metrics offer insights into the resource utilization of each container, allowing operations teams to detect inefficiencies, optimize resource allocation, and ensure the seamless functioning of applications.

Alongside performance metrics, monitoring tools can also track events within the Docker environment. These events, such as the starting or stopping of containers, offer a chronological view of container activity. By correlating events with performance metrics, teams can ascertain the cause-and-effect relationships. For instance, a spike in CPU usage can be traced back to a specific container's start event, thereby helping identify rogue processes or resource-intensive tasks.

While monitoring offers a real-time view of the Docker environment, logging complements it by providing a historical record of container activity. Logs are the textual records generated by applications, systems, and platforms. In the context of Docker, logs can emanate from multiple sources, including the Docker daemon, individual containers, and even orchestrators like Kubernetes or Docker Swarm. These logs are instrumental in troubleshooting, offering a detailed view of application behavior, errors, and system messages.

Docker, inherently, provides mechanisms for both monitoring and logging. The Docker API exposes endpoints that can be queried to obtain container metrics. Additionally, Docker's native logging drivers, like 'json-file' or 'journald,' capture container logs, making them accessible via the 'docker logs' command. However, in large-scale deployments, relying solely on Docker's native capabilities can be limiting. This is where third-party monitoring and logging solutions come into play.

Prometheus, for instance, has emerged as a widespread monitoring solution in containerized environments. Integrated with Docker, Prometheus can scrape metrics from the Docker daemon and containers, providing a centralized dashboard for visualization. Grafana, often used in tandem with Prometheus, enhances visualization capabilities, allowing teams to create custom dashboards tailored to specific needs.

On the logging front, solutions like the ELK Stack (Elasticsearch, Logstash, Kibana) or EFK Stack (Elasticsearch, Fluentd, Kibana) have gained prominence. These solutions aggregate logs from various sources, index them for faster searches, and provide visualization tools for log analysis. In Docker environments, log shippers like Fluentd or Logstash can be deployed as containers, capturing logs from other containers and forwarding them to a centralized logging backend like Elasticsearch.

Beyond tooling, Docker's successful monitoring and logging strategy hinges on best practices. Given the voluminous nature of logs and metrics in large deployments, it's essential to prioritize. Not every log message or metric warrants attention. By establishing logging levels and monitoring thresholds, teams can filter out the noise, focusing on anomalies or critical messages. Regularly pruning and rotating logs ensure that storage is used efficiently, and older logs don't consume unnecessary space.

Security, often at the forefront of operational concerns, is also pivotal in monitoring and logging. Ensuring that monitoring tools have restricted access, employing encryption for logs in transit and at rest, and masking sensitive data within logs are all practices that safeguard against potential security threats.

In conclusion, as Docker solidifies its position as a cornerstone of modern software deployment, mastering monitoring and logging becomes non-negotiable for operations teams. These activities, far from being mere operational chores, are the eyes and ears of the team, offering insights, aiding in troubleshooting, and ensuring the optimal performance of containerized applications. By leveraging both Docker's native capabilities and third-party solutions, and by adhering to best practices, teams can ensure that their Docker environments are not just efficient but also resilient and secure.

CHAPTER XI

Popular Use Cases of Docker

Setting up Development Environments

The software development ecosystem has continuously evolved over the decades, adapting to emerging technological advancements and best practices. Once plagued by the infamous "it works on my machine" syndrome, traditional development methods often led to inconsistencies and unforeseen issues when software was deployed in different environments. The introduction of Docker into the software realm heralded a transformative approach to setting up development environments, ensuring consistency, scalability, and reproducibility. This section explores the nuances and advantages of leveraging Docker to craft development environments, guiding readers through its transformative impact and practical applications.

Docker's foundational principle lies in containerization. Containers are lightweight, stand-alone packages that encapsulate an application and its entire runtime environment, including libraries, binaries, and configuration files. By abstracting the underlying infrastructure, Docker containers ensure that an application runs consistently, irrespective of where the container is deployed. This intrinsic consistency has profound implications when applied to development environments, effectively eliminating disparities between development, testing, staging, and production setups.

In the pre-Docker era, setting up a development environment was often tedious. Developers would painstakingly configure their local machines, installing necessary libraries, dependencies, databases, and other services. This manual configuration, apart from being time-consuming, often led to discrepancies, as two developers might have slightly different setups, leading to unpredictable behavior when the software was integrated or deployed. Docker, with its container-centric approach, provides a solution to this problem. Instead of configuring a local machine directly, developers set up Docker containers tailored to their application's needs. Given their consistent and isolated nature, these containers ensure that every developer works in a mirror image of the production environment.

Setting up a development environment in Docker typically starts with defining a Dockerfile. This file, a blueprint of the container, delineates instructions on which base image to use (e.g., a Python or Node.js environment), what software packages to install, how to copy the application source code into the container, and other configuration details. With the Dockerfile in place, developers use the docker build command to generate a Docker image, which can then be instantiated into a running container using docker run. This process ensures that every aspect of the environment, from the operating system to the application's configuration, is codified, versioned, and reproducible.

A significant boon of Docker-based development environments is their composability. Often, applications don't run in isolation; they interact with databases, caching systems, messaging queues, and other services. Docker Compose, a tool integrated with Docker, allows developers to define multi-container applications easily. Using a docker-compose.yml file, developers can specify various services their application requires and configurations. For instance, a web application might need a Node.js container for its backend, a PostgreSQL container for its database, and a Redis container for caching. Docker Compose allows all these services to be defined, linked, and managed as a cohesive unit, ensuring that developers have a holistic environment closely mirroring production setups.

While the advantages of Docker in setting up development environments are manifold, it's also essential to understand its transformative impact on the broader development workflow. Continuous Integration (CI) and Continuous Deployment (CD) are pillars of modern software delivery practices. Docker's inherent consistency ensures that software tested within a Docker container on a developer's machine will behave the same when tested in a CI pipeline or when deployed to production. This congruence reduces the chances of unexpected errors, leading to quicker and more reliable software releases.

Additionally, Docker's ecosystem offers a wealth of pre-configured images via Docker Hub, its public repository. Whether a developer needs a specific version of Python, a pre-configured Jupyter Notebook setup, or a LAMP (Linux, Apache, MySQL, PHP) stack, Docker Hub likely has an image ready to be pulled and used. This extensive library further simplifies setting up development environments, often reducing the setup to a single docker pull command.

However, it's also crucial to address challenges and best practices. One should not treat Docker containers as lightweight Virtual Machines; they're ephemeral by nature. Therefore, understanding how to manage data persistence, network configurations, and container orchestration becomes crucial as complex projects grow. Moreover, while Docker does provide isolation, developers should be conscious of security best practices, regularly updating base images to patch vulnerabilities and using trusted images from reputable sources.

In conclusion, Docker's foray into software development has redefined how development environments are perceived and configured. Gone are the days of laboriously setting up local machines and grappling with unforeseen environment-related issues. With Docker, consistency, reproducibility, and scalability are woven into the fabric of development processes. By understanding Docker's principles and harnessing its tools effectively, developers can streamline their workflows and foster a culture of collaborative development, where code is seamlessly integrated, tested, and deployed, paving the way for more robust and reliable software solutions.

Continuous Integration/Continuous Deployment (CI/CD)
In the dynamic world of software development, the quest for efficiency, reliability, and speed is unending. The Continuous

Integration and Continuous Deployment methodologies rise, which revolve around the principles of automation and consistent integration of code changes, has been central to this pursuit. Docker, with its robust capabilities for containerization, has augmented the CI/CD landscape, offering a delivery paradigm where software changes are integrated and tested continuously and packaged and deployed in a consistent environment. This section delves deep into the interplay of CI/CD and Docker, exploring this amalgamation's transformative effects and inherent advantages.

The first step in grasping the essence of CI/CD in Docker is to understand the individual components. Continuous Integration (CI) emphasizes the importance of integrating code changes from multiple contributors into a shared repository multiple times a day. These integrations are automatically verified through automated builds and tests, ensuring errors and bugs are detected early. Continuous Deployment (CD), on the other hand, takes this a step further. Once the code passes through the CI phase, it is automatically distributed to the production environment without manual intervention, ensuring the software delivery process is agile and consistent.

Enter Docker, a technology built on the principle of containerization. A Docker container packages an application and its required environment, including system libraries, binaries, and configurations. This packaged environment ensures that the application behaves consistently irrespective of where the container is launched. Predictability and consistency are priceless in a CI/CD pipeline, where code must transition smoothly through various stages, from integration and testing to staging and production.

Docker's synergy with CI/CD begins with its Dockerfile—a blueprint for creating Docker images. Developers create Dockerfiles to specify the environment in which their application should run. This includes the base operating system, necessary software packages, and application configurations. When changes are pushed to a repository, the CI system can use this Dockerfile to build a fresh Docker image. This image then serves as the foundation for all subsequent testing, ensuring that tests run in the same environment where the application will eventually be deployed.

The CI phase, thus, benefits immensely from Docker. Traditional CI systems, without containerization, would often run into the notorious "it works on my machine" problem, where code that worked perfectly on a developer's local setup would inexplicably fail in the CI environment due to subtle environment differences. With Docker, this issue is virtually eliminated. Every time code is integrated, it's tested inside a consistent Docker container, ensuring environment uniformity from a developer's local machine to production.

The CD phase, which focuses on deployment, is where Docker's capabilities truly shine. Containers encapsulate not just the application, but also its environment. This means that when an application is ready to be deployed after passing the CI tests, it isn't just the code that's deployed. Instead, the entire Docker container is deployed with the application and its precise environment. This leads to an unprecedented level of consistency in deployments. Gone are the days when developers had to ensure that the production environment matched the development environment painstakingly. With Docker, the application's environment is inherently a part of its package.

Moreover, Docker complements modern orchestration tools like Kubernetes, which are designed to handle the deployment, scaling, and management of containerized applications. Such orchestrators ensure that Docker containers resulting from the CI/CD process are seamlessly deployed, maintained, and scaled in production clusters. They can roll out updates with zero downtime, rollback problematic deployments, and ensure high availability—a testament to the symbiotic relationship between Docker, CI/CD, and container orchestration.

There are practical considerations, too. Docker Hub, Docker's public repository, integrates well with popular CI/CD tools like Jenkins, Travis CI, and GitLab CI. This means that CI/CD pipelines can easily pull base images, build new images, run tests inside containers, and push production-ready images to repositories, all in an automated manner. Such integrations drastically simplify the CI/CD setup and reduce the possibility of human error.

While the benefits are manifold, it's also crucial to address challenges. The transient nature of containers implies that data persistence needs special attention. Developers must ensure that databases or any other stateful parts of an application are handled correctly during continuous deployments. Additionally, security cannot be an afterthought. Automated pipelines should include security checks, scanning Docker images for vulnerabilities, and ensuring that only trusted images are used.

In conclusion, the fusion of Docker with CI/CD methodologies represents a watershed moment in software delivery. By marrying the consistency and isolation of Docker containers with the automation and agility of CI/CD, developers can now assure faster, more reliable, and incredibly consistent software releases. In order to ensure that the finished product is greater than the sum of its parts, the future of software delivery therefore involves more than just developing code. It involves utilizing tools and processes that can seamlessly integrate, test, package, and deploy this code. In the future, Docker and CI/CD are not just tools but vanguards leading the charge.

Microservices Architecture

In software development, where paradigms and tools constantly evolve, specific ideas strike a chord so deeply that they bring about foundational shifts. One such revolutionary idea has been the concept of "Microservices Architecture" which, combined with Docker's power, paves the way for scalable, robust, and efficient software applications. This section explores the profound relationship between microservices and Docker, detailing how they synergize to redefine our understanding of application design and deployment.

At the heart of the microservices architecture lies a simple yet transformative principle: decomposing an application into small, loosely coupled services that run as separate entities but work in concert to deliver a unified application experience. Instead of building a monolithic application, where all components are interwoven and run in a single process, microservices advocate for creating independent services that are responsible for specific business functionalities. Each service has its own data store, runs in its own process, and communicates with others using lightweight mechanisms, often HTTP-based APIs.

This decentralized approach provides myriad benefits. Firstly, each service can be developed, deployed, and scaled independently. If a specific functionality of an application experiences heavy traffic, only its corresponding service needs to be scaled, rather than the entire application. This granular scalability not only makes applications more responsive to demands but also more cost-effective. Secondly, as each service is independent, teams can develop them in parallel, using the programming languages and tools best suited for the task, leading to faster development cycles. Additionally, since these services are loosely coupled, failures in one service are less likely to cascade and bring down the entire application.

However, microservices offer these compelling advantages but also introduce complexities, primarily concerning service deployment, communication, and management. This is where Docker enters the picture, turning potential challenges into streamlined solutions.

Docker's core strength is containerization. A Docker container packages an application and its entire runtime environment—libraries, binaries, and configuration files—into a single unit. This ensures the application runs consistently, regardless of where the container is deployed. For microservices, each service, irrespective of its underlying technology stack, can be containerized and run independently. This encapsulation ensures consistency across development, testing, and production environments, resolving the age-old dilemma of "it works on my machine."

When deploying microservices using Docker, each service gets its container. These containers can be started, stopped, and replicated independently, providing a perfect match for the inherent nature of microservices. If a particular service needs to be updated, its container can be replaced without affecting other services. This leads to minimal downtime, faster rollbacks, and the flexibility to adopt a continuous deployment approach.

Docker also shines in microservices' networking. By default, Docker containers can interact with each other, but they remain isolated from the host system. Using Docker's networking capabilities, developers can create custom networks, allowing specific containers (or services) to communicate while keeping others isolated. This is important because it makes sure that microservices may easily communicate to one another while yet being very secure.

Moreover, Docker supports service discovery out of the box. Service discovery becomes pivotal in a microservices environment where services need to locate and communicate with each other. With tools like Docker Swarm and integration capabilities with orchestrators like Kubernetes, Docker simplifies this process, allowing services to register themselves and discover others dynamically.

Data persistence is another area where Docker complements microservices. Given that each microservice can have its data store, Docker offers volumes and bind mounts, ensuring that data remains persistent even if containers are restarted. This ensures that stateful services, like databases or caches, can be reliably run within Docker containers without the risk of data loss.

Orchestration, a necessity in a microservices setup due to the sheer number of services running concurrently, is another area where Docker excels, especially when combined with tools like Kubernetes or Docker Swarm. These orchestrators handle deployment, scaling, and management of containerized applications, ensuring that the right number of containers are running, services are load-balanced, and failures are automatically recovered.

Despite the undeniable benefits, developers must approach the Docker-microservices combination with a well-thought-out strategy. Microservices, though powerful, can lead to increased complexity due to the need to manage inter-service communication, handle data consistency, and maintain service boundaries. While it simplifies deployment, Docker requires a solid understanding of container management, especially in production environments.

In conclusion, the confluence of microservices and Docker represents a powerful shift in the software development landscape. Organizations can achieve unparalleled scalability, resilience, and agility by deconstructing applications into small, focused services and leveraging Docker's containerization capabilities. The future of software, thus, lies not in monolithic designs but in adaptive, distributed architectures that harness the strengths of both microservices and Docker. The combination promises a new way to design applications and a more resilient, scalable, and agile future for software deployment and management.

CHAPTER XII

Docker Ecosystem

Docker Hub and Docker Store

As we advance deeper into the containerization era, understanding and efficiently leveraging tools and platforms built around Docker becomes paramount. At its core, Docker provides a method to package, distribute, and manage applications consistently across various environments. To bolster this capability and provide a unified platform for sharing and distribution, Docker introduced two pivotal repositories: Docker Hub and Docker Store. This section delves into the intricacies of these two platforms, unraveling their significance in the Docker ecosystem.

At first glance, both Docker Hub and Docker Store might seem similar, primarily serving as repositories for Docker images. However, diving deeper reveals distinct functionalities, purposes, and target audiences for each platform. Understanding these nuances is essential for anyone engaged in container-based application development, deployment, or orchestration.

Docker Hub can be best described as the GitHub for Docker images. It's a cloud-based registry service that allows developers to link code repositories, build details, and more into a comprehensive automated workflow. In simpler terms, Docker Hub is a centralized platform where developers can create, test, store, and distribute container images.

One of Docker Hub's flagship features is its automated build process. Developers can link their GitHub or Bitbucket repositories to Docker Hub. Whenever there's a code update in the linked repository, Docker Hub automatically triggers a new build, creating a fresh Docker image. This seamless integration and automation significantly enhance the Continuous Integration and Continuous Deployment pipeline, ensuring that the latest version of an application is always containerized and ready for deployment.

Furthermore, Docker Hub serves as a communal platform, fostering open-source collaboration. Developers worldwide can share their Docker images for general utilities, specific tools, or complex applications. This public sharing capability has led to a rich library of Docker images available to all, accelerating application development and deployment. Instead of creating a Docker image from scratch, developers can pull an existing image from Docker Hub, modify it to their requirements, and then use it. This capability has made Docker Hub an indispensable asset for the Docker community.

In addition to public repositories, Docker Hub also supports private repositories, catering to businesses and individual developers who wish to keep their Docker images confidential. These private repositories ensure that the Docker images stored are only accessible to authorized users, providing an added layer of security.

While Docker Hub is geared primarily toward developers and open-source communities, Docker Store is aimed at enterprises. It's a platform where software vendors, community contributors, and businesses can share and procure containerized software. What sets Docker Store apart from Docker Hub is its emphasis on verified, enterprise-ready containers.

Every Docker image on the Docker Store undergoes a rigorous vetting process. This ensures that the containerized software is secure, free from vulnerabilities, and optimized for performance. For businesses, this means reducing the risk associated with deploying third-party containers. They can be confident that any container procured from Docker Store meets a high standard of quality and security.

Another distinguishing feature of Docker Store is its support for commercial software. Vendors can sell their software as Docker containers, providing businesses a streamlined way to purchase and deploy commercial applications. This benefits vendors by providing them with a platform to reach a wider audience and aids businesses by offering a centralized marketplace to procure enterprise-ready software.

Moreover, Docker Store integrates seamlessly with Docker Datacenter, Docker's enterprise container platform. This ensures businesses can smoothly integrate any containerized software procured from the Docker Store into their existing Docker-based infrastructure.

While Docker Hub and Docker Store serve distinct audiences, their coexistence is not mutually exclusive. In many scenarios, a Docker image might start its journey on Docker Hub, shared by a developer or a community. Once it gains traction and undergoes further optimization and security enhancements, the same image might find its way to the Docker Store as an enterprise-ready container.

In conclusion, both Docker Hub and Docker Store play pivotal roles in the Docker ecosystem. Docker Hub, emphasizing open-source collaboration, automated builds, and CI/CD integration, empowers developers to create, share, and distribute Docker images effortlessly. On the other hand, Docker Store, with its rigorous vetting process and support for commercial software, serves as a trusted marketplace for businesses seeking enterprise-ready containerized applications.

In a world rapidly embracing containerization, these platforms not only provide tools and resources for effective Docker image management but also foster a community where knowledge, tools, and applications are shared, discussed, and enhanced. Through Docker Hub and Docker Store, Docker Inc. has ensured that whether you're an individual developer, an open-source contributor, or a large enterprise, there's a platform tailored to your Docker image needs.

Introduction to Kubernetes

In today's technology-driven landscape, how applications are developed, deployed, and scaled has significantly transformed. Containers have revolutionized application deployment with their promise of portability, consistency, and efficiency. However, as the container ecosystem matured, a new challenge emerged: how do you efficiently manage, orchestrate, and scale hundreds or even thousands of containers? This is where Kubernetes, an open-source container orchestration platform, comes into play. In this section, we will explore the foundational concepts of Kubernetes, its architectural design, and why it stands out in the complex world of container orchestration.

Kubernetes, often called by its Greek name K8s, originated from a project at Google called 'Borg.' It was Google's solution to manage and orchestrate its vast number of containers. Recognizing the universal challenges associated with container management, Google open-sourced the project in 2014, entrusting its evolution to the Cloud Native Computing Foundation (CNCF). Since then, Kubernetes has grown exponentially in popularity, becoming the de-facto standard for container orchestration.

So, what exactly does Kubernetes do? At a high level, Kubernetes automates containerized applications' deployment, scaling, and management. It provides a framework to run containers resiliently, ensuring high availability, failover capabilities, and zero-downtime deployments. Beyond this, Kubernetes introduces a set of abstractions and APIs that make managing containerized workloads and services easier and more intuitive.

The architecture of Kubernetes is both robust and modular. It comprises a cluster, which is the fundamental operating unit and can be visualized as a single entity. A cluster has at least one master node and multiple worker nodes. The master node houses the Kubernetes control plane components, which are responsible for governing the Kubernetes cluster. This includes the API server, which serves as the entry point for commands; the etcd, a consistent and highly-available key-value store for all cluster data; the scheduler, which assigns work, in the form of containers, to worker nodes; and the controller manager, which regulates controllers ensuring the desired state of the system.

On the other hand, Worker nodes are the powerhouses where the containers and workloads run. Each worker node contains a Kubelet, a tiny application communicating with the master node, ensuring the containers are running as expected. They also host services like the Docker runtime, responsible for running the actual containers, and Kube Proxy, which maintains network rules for container communication.

Kubernetes introduces several powerful abstractions, each serving a distinct purpose. The smallest deployable units in Kubernetes, known as "pods," have the capacity to hold one or more containers. A pod's containers may communicate effectively with one another since they have the same IP, port space, and storage. 'Services' in Kubernetes provide a stable IP address and DNS name to a set of pods, automatically load-balancing traffic across them. 'Volumes' offer persistent pod storage solutions, ensuring data remains intact even if the container restarts. Furthermore, entities like 'ReplicaSets' ensure that a specified number of pod replicas run at any given time, and 'Deployments' facilitate declarative updates for pods and replica sets.

Why has Kubernetes gained such widespread acclaim in the tech community? The reasons are multifaceted. Kubernetes provides a unified API, enabling it to manage and orchestrate containers irrespective of the underlying infrastructure, be it on-premises servers or cloud providers like AWS, Azure, or Google Cloud. It brings resilience and fault tolerance to applications, ensuring they remain accessible even if specific components fail. Kubernetes' ability to auto-scale applications, based on metrics like CPU usage or HTTP traffic, ensures resources are utilized efficiently and applications can handle varying loads. Additionally, its rich ecosystem, supported by a vast community of developers, has created tools, extensions, and integrations that enhance and simplify Kubernetes functionalities.

However, it's essential to note that Kubernetes is not without its complexities. Setting up and managing a Kubernetes cluster, especially at scale, can be challenging. Concepts like service discovery, ingress control, and stateful application management can be daunting for newcomers. Thankfully, managed Kubernetes services, offered by cloud providers, abstract away much of the underlying complexities, allowing users to leverage Kubernetes' capabilities without diving deep into its intricacies.

In conclusion, Kubernetes has undeniably reshaped the landscape of container management and orchestration. Its robust architecture and powerful abstractions provide an unparalleled platform to run containerized applications resiliently. While Kubernetes has a learning curve, its efficiency, scalability, and resilience benefits make it an invaluable tool for modern application deployment. As the world of containers continues to evolve, Kubernetes stands as a testament to what is achievable when robust engineering meets the challenges of modern-day application requirements.

CHAPTER XIII

Troubleshooting Common Docker Issues

Dealing with Container Errors

The revolutionary rise of container technology has undeniably transformed how developers build, test, and deploy applications. Containers have gained an immense following in recent years, offering portability, consistency, and resource efficiency. However, as with all technologies, working with containers is challenging. Errors can emerge at any phase, from building an image to running a container in production. This section delves into the intricacies of container errors, exploring common pitfalls, their root causes, and best practices for resolution.

At their core, containers encapsulate an application and its dependencies into a single unit, guaranteeing consistency across various environments. This encapsulation is facilitated by container engines like Docker, which create and run containers from images. But herein lies the first realm of potential errors: image creation. When creating a Docker image from a Dockerfile, developers can encounter issues like unsatisfied dependencies, missing files, or incorrect commands. These issues often manifest as build errors. It's crucial to have a comprehensive understanding of the base image being used and to ensure that the instructions in the Dockerfile are accurate and sequential. Debugging at this stage often requires meticulously reviewing the Dockerfile, checking each command, and validating the required dependencies.

Once an image is successfully built, the next phase is running a container from that image. This stage can be riddled with errors related to configuration. For instance, if a containerized application expects certain environment variables to be set, but they're missing, it might fail to start. Port binding errors are another common nuisance. Containers communicate with the external world through ports, and if a required port is already in use or not correctly mapped, the container might crash. Furthermore, data persistence and volume-related errors can plague developers. If a container expects a specific volume to be mounted, but it isn't, data inconsistencies or loss can occur.

Another challenge is managing container resources. Containers run in isolated environments with allocated CPU, memory, and other resources. If a container exceeds its allocated memory, it's terminated, leading to the infamous "Out of Memory" error. Likewise, if a container tries to consume more CPU than allocated, it can be throttled, leading to performance issues. Properly configuring resource limits and constantly monitoring container resource usage are paramount to avoiding these pitfalls.

In clustered, orchestrated environments like Kubernetes, the complexities multiply. Here, containers are often grouped into pods, which are managed and scaled based on configurations and policies. A common issue in such settings is the 'CrashLoopBackOff' state. This error indicates that a container in a pod is repeatedly crashing after start. The reasons can range from configuration errors, unsatisfied dependencies, to resource constraints. Diagnosing such issues requires checking pod logs, describing pod states, and even sometimes diving deep into the application code.

Networking errors are another frequent grievance in orchestrated environments. Containers within a pod can communicate seamlessly, but inter-pod communication requires proper network configurations. If services, which expose pods to network traffic, are misconfigured, it can lead to unreachable applications. Similarly, ingress controllers, which manage external access to services in a cluster, can be sources of errors if not correctly set up. Debugging these requires a deep dive into network policies, service configurations, and ingress rules.

However, identifying and diagnosing errors is just one part of the equation. The next crucial step is error prevention and building resilient containerized applications. Employing best practices can significantly reduce the occurrence of errors. For starters, always use trusted and minimal base images for containers. This reduces the attack surface and ensures that only necessary components are present. Regularly updating and scanning these images for vulnerabilities is equally essential.

For configurations, especially in orchestrated environments, employing tools that validate configurations before deployment can be a lifesaver. Tools like kube-score or kubeval can analyze Kubernetes configurations and highlight potential issues. Likewise, setting up proper monitoring and logging solutions can provide real-time insights into container health. Solutions like Prometheus for monitoring and Fluentd or ELK stack for logging can offer invaluable information when things go awry.

Lastly, it's essential to understand that errors and challenges are part and parcel of evolving technologies. The key is to approach them with a systematic mindset. Containers, though transformative, are not silver bullets. They come with their own set of challenges that require continuous learning, adaptation, and resilience. Debugging and resolving errors in containerized environments necessitate a blend of understanding the underlying technology, the application, and a pinch of intuition. But with each fixed error, the system grows more robust, and the developer more seasoned.

In conclusion, as the world increasingly embraces containers and orchestrated environments, understanding potential pitfalls and effectively dealing with container errors becomes pivotal. Through a combination of best practices, monitoring, logging, and continuous learning, developers and system administrators can navigate the intricate maze of container errors, ensuring robust, scalable, and efficient application deployments.

Network and Volume-related Issues

The world of containers has reinvented the wheel of application deployment, ensuring that software runs reliably when moved from one computing environment to another. Such is the power of Docker and similar technologies, where an application and its environment are bundled into a singular unit – the container. However, as with all technologies, the rose comes with thorns. Two of the most intricate challenges faced in container orchestration relate to networks and volumes. Understanding the nuances of these components and their associated issues is pivotal for developers and administrators who wish to harness containerization's power fully.

Networks are the highways that ferry data between applications, services, and users. In a containerized environment, this network is a complex web interlinking multiple containers, potentially across numerous hosts. The primary role of Docker's networking is to establish communication between containers, and between containers and external networks. Docker offers several networking modes: bridge, host, overlay, and macvlan, each with its own use case and potential pitfalls.

The default network mode is 'bridge,' and challenges are uncommon to arise here. One recurrent problem is IP address conflict. If Docker's default IP range for bridge mode conflicts with the host's network range, it could lead to connectivity issues. Adjusting Docker's default bridge network is often the solution, but it requires diving deep into configuration files.

Another commonly faced network issue is port conflicts. Containers interact with external systems via ports. If two containers are incorrectly configured to use the same port or if a container tries to bind to a port already in use on the host system, it can result in binding errors.

In multi-host environments, overlay networks come into play. They allow containers spread across multiple hosts to communicate. However, this brings a whole new set of challenges. Overlay networks rely on a distributed key-value store, like etcd or Consul, and any issues with these systems can lead to network failures. Additionally, firewall configurations, host network settings, and even time synchronization problems between hosts can lead to failures in overlay network creation.

While networks manage the data in transit, volumes handle data at rest. They are Docker's solution to the transient nature of containers. Volumes allow data to persist beyond a container's life and are also used to share data between containers.

One frequent volume-related challenge is the loss of data upon container termination. This usually stems from a misunderstanding of Docker's storage mechanics. Unlike bind mounts and tmpfs mounts, named volumes are designed to persist data. An error in configuring or choosing the right mount type can lead to data vanishing when a container is terminated.

Permissions pose another substantial hurdle. When volumes are mounted, they often retain the permissions and ownership of the host system, which might not align with the container's user. This can lead to situations where a container might not have the necessary permissions to read or write to a mounted volume, causing application failures.

Data consistency is another realm of potential pitfalls. In scenarios where multiple containers share a single volume, and both containers write data to it, ensuring data consistency becomes crucial. This can lead to data corruption or overwrites without the right configurations or mechanisms.

Misconfigurations, especially when dealing with Docker Compose or orchestration tools like Kubernetes, can also be a source of volume-related problems. An incorrect path, a missing volume declaration, or even a typo in a configuration file can prevent volumes from being correctly mounted, leading to application errors.

A systematic approach to troubleshooting can prove invaluable for network and volume-related issues. Starting with logs is always a good idea. Docker provides detailed logs, and tools like docker inspect can offer insights into network and volume configurations of running or terminated containers.

For network issues, utilities like ping, netstat, and traceroute can assist in diagnosing connectivity problems. Ensuring that the distributed key-value store is healthy and correctly configured when dealing with overlay networks is crucial.

For volume issues, starting with permissions is a prudent approach. Checking and comparing the host's permissions with the container's user can resolve many problems. Furthermore, understanding and choosing the right type of storage – named volumes, bind mounts, or tmpfs mounts – based on the use case is paramount.

Regular backups are a non-negotiable best practice when it comes to volumes. Data corruption or loss is possible even with the best configurations, and regular backups can be a safety net.

Lastly, automation can be a savior. Using Infrastructure as Code (IAC) tools can ensure that configurations are consistent and reproducible, reducing the scope for manual errors. Also, monitoring tools that provide real-time metrics and alerts on network and volume status can be the first defense against potential issues.

Containers have undeniably revolutionized the way we think about software deployment. But with great power comes great responsibility. The intricacies of network and volume-related issues in Docker can be daunting, but with a deep understanding, systematic troubleshooting, and best practices, they are navigable. As containerization continues to be a cornerstone of modern software infrastructure, mastering these challenges becomes beneficial and essential.

Resources and Monitoring

In the fascinating world of containerization, the capacity to run applications consistently across different environments is truly revolutionary. Docker, being at the forefront of this movement, provides not just the platform to create and run containers, but also a sophisticated system to manage resources and monitor the health of containers. This intricate process of managing resources and constant vigilance ensures that the system runs optimally, and applications deliver their intended performance. Diving deep into the realms of resources and monitoring in Docker gives us insights into how crucial these aspects are for seamless and efficient container orchestration.

Every application requires resources: CPU, memory, I/O, and network bandwidth, to name the most critical. Containers, encapsulating an application and its environment, also need these resources. Managing these resources becomes a delicate balancing act in a system where numerous containers might be running simultaneously.

By default, Docker does not impose stringent resource limits, which can lead to situations where one container could potentially hog all available resources, thereby stifling others. This is where resource constraints come into play. Docker provides mechanisms to assign specific amounts of memory, CPU shares, disk I/O, and network bandwidth to containers, ensuring that no single container can run rampant at the expense of others.

Memory limits are of paramount importance. Containers exceeding their memory limits can be automatically restarted or even terminated, depending on the configuration. By setting a memory reservation and a hard limit, Docker can ensure that a container always has a memory baseline available, but cannot exceed its upper boundary.

Similarly, CPU shares are pivotal in ensuring computational fairness. Docker uses a relative weight system for CPU allocation. Every container gets an equal share by default, but developers can assign more shares to specific containers if required. This doesn't limit a container's CPU usage but dictates its proportion with others.

I/O, both disk and network, can also be throttled in Docker. By setting I/O limits, one can ensure that data-intensive containers do not overwhelm the system, thereby ensuring smoother overall performance.

Resource management is not just about setting limits. It also involves ensuring that containers can access enough resources to function optimally. This often requires a keen understanding of the application's needs and a constant tuning process to strike the right balance.

While resource management sets the stage, monitoring is the ever-watchful sentinel, ensuring that everything operates within expected parameters. Monitoring in Docker is multifaceted, spanning container performance, resource usage, application health, and more.

At the basic level, Docker provides native tools that offer insights into containers. The docker stats command, for instance, provides a real-time stream of resource usage metrics – CPU, memory, I/O, and network stats, for all running containers. This is the first line of defense in monitoring, offering a bird's eye view of the system.

However, for deeper insights, more sophisticated tools come into play. Platforms like Prometheus, integrated with Grafana for visualization, provide detailed metrics about container health and performance. They can offer granular data, from the CPU usage of a single container to the network traffic patterns over extended periods.

Application performance monitoring (APM) tools, like New Relic or Datadog, can dive even more profound, focusing on the applications running within containers. They provide insights into application behavior, response times, error rates, and transaction traces. Such tools are invaluable in microservices architectures, where multiple containerized services might be interacting, and identifying bottlenecks or errors can be like finding a needle in a haystack.

Log management is another facet of monitoring. Containers, mainly when orchestrated using platforms like Kubernetes, can be ephemeral, with lifetimes ranging from seconds to days. Persisting logs, therefore, becomes crucial. Solutions like the ELK stack (Elasticsearch, Logstash, Kibana) or Loki can aggregate logs from containers, ensuring they are available for analysis long after the container has terminated.

Alerting completes the monitoring picture. It's not feasible to have human eyes on dashboards 24/7. Alerting mechanisms can be configured to notify teams when specific thresholds are breached or anomalies detected. This proactive approach ensures that potential issues can be addressed before they escalate into full-blown crises.

Resource management and monitoring are deeply interconnected. Without effective resource management, containers could run into performance issues, leading to application errors or system instability. Conversely, without vigilant monitoring, one cannot ascertain if the resources allocated are being used optimally or if adjustments are required.

The tuning of resource allocations based on monitoring insights is an ongoing process. As applications evolve and as traffic patterns change, the resource needs of containers will also shift. Monitoring provides the data required to make informed decisions, ensuring the system remains resilient and efficient.

In the vast orchestra of container orchestration, resources and monitoring are like the conductor, ensuring every instrument (container) plays its part perfectly. They ensure harmony, balance, and optimal performance in a world where consistency and reliability are paramount. As Docker and container technologies continue to dominate the software deployment landscape, mastering the art of resource management and the science of monitoring becomes indispensable for organizations and developers alike.

CHAPTER XIV

Looking Forward- The Future of Docker and Containerization

Ongoing Developments in the Docker World

The realm of technology is dynamic, characterized by continuous change and adaptation. As a significant component of the contemporary software landscape, the Docker ecosystem isn't exempt from this whirlwind of innovation. Since its inception in 2013, Docker has revolutionized how applications are developed, shipped, and deployed, giving rise to the age of containerization. As we delve into the ongoing developments in the Docker world, we're reminded of the boundless possibilities that lay ahead and how Docker continues to shape the future of software development and deployment.

Understanding the ongoing developments in Docker requires a brief look at its evolutionary trajectory. Docker began as a project focused on providing lightweight, isolated environments (containers) for running applications. It promised and delivered consistency across multiple platforms and environments, from a developer's workstation to a production server. This key feature garnered immediate attention, making Docker synonymous with containerization.

As Docker gained traction, the ecosystem around it flourished. The introduction of Docker Hub, a repository for sharing and distributing container images, further bolstered Docker's position. Over the years, Docker Swarm was introduced as a native clustering and orchestration solution, Docker Compose facilitated multi-container application deployments, and Docker Enterprise brought containerization to large enterprises.

One of the most significant ongoing developments in Docker's journey is its embrace of Kubernetes. Initially, Docker and Kubernetes were seen as competitors, with Docker Swarm and Kubernetes both vying for the orchestration crown. However, recognizing the growing popularity and community support for Kubernetes, Docker decided to integrate Kubernetes support into its platform.

Docker's integration with Kubernetes isn't merely a surface-level addition. Docker has invested in making Kubernetes a first-class citizen within its ecosystem. The recent versions of Docker Desktop come with Kubernetes built-in, allowing developers to initiate a Kubernetes cluster with a single click. This seamless integration lowers the entry barrier for many developers wanting to experiment with Kubernetes without diving deep into its complexities.

Docker has always been about developers. Recognizing the changing needs and preferences of the developer community, Docker has been consistently enhancing its tooling and platform. Docker Desktop's enhancements are a testament to this commitment. With features like GUI-based container management, real-time logs viewer, and the ability to quickly switch contexts between different orchestration platforms, Docker simplifies container development.

Furthermore, Docker's recent efforts in simplifying multi-container applications are noteworthy. With the evolution of microservices architectures, developers often grapple with running multiple interconnected containers locally. Docker Compose, while already a robust tool, is receiving enhancements to handle complex application architectures better, further simplifying the developer experience.

As container adoption grows, so do security concerns. Containers, by their isolated nature, already offer a level of security. However, as recent events in the tech world have shown, no system is infallible. Recognizing the critical importance of security, Docker has been at the forefront of introducing security-centric features.

Docker Content Trust, introduced a few years ago, was a significant step in this direction. It provides image signing and verification, ensuring that the images being used are genuine and unaltered. Ongoing developments see Docker working on runtime security, scanning for image vulnerabilities, and offering tighter integration with enterprise security systems.

Docker's ecosystem is vast and growing. As the central repository for container images, Docker Hub continues to see enhancements aimed at better organization, security, and discovery of images. But

Docker's ecosystem isn't limited to Docker Hub. Docker Store, introduced to provide enterprise-grade container images, plugins, and extensions, is seeing a continuous influx of tools and solutions.

The plugin architecture of Docker is another area of focus. Docker realizes that while its platform is robust, the broader community can offer further integrations and features to enhance the experience. By providing a rich plugin architecture, Docker ensures that third-party developers and vendors can seamlessly integrate their solutions, making Docker more versatile.

Open source lies at the heart of Docker. Recognizing the strength of the community, Docker has been fostering collaborations. The Moby Project, initiated by Docker, is a testament to this collaborative spirit. It's an open framework, allowing the community to assemble specialized container systems without transforming the wheel. This initiative ensures that while Docker continues its focused journey on enhancing its core platform, the broader community can leverage the components Docker has developed to create tailored solutions.

While Docker has made monumental strides, the journey is far from over. The world of containers is evolving, with new use cases emerging, from edge computing to AI/ML workloads. Docker is poised to grow with these changing needs.

Edge computing, characterized by running applications closer to data sources like IoT devices, presents unique challenges. Docker's lightweight nature makes it apt for such scenarios, and ongoing developments aim to make Docker an integral part of the edge computing revolution.

In the realm of AI and ML, the reproducibility of environments is crucial. Docker's ability to provide consistent environments makes it a natural fit for AI/ML workloads. Recognizing this synergy, Docker is enhancing its platform to better cater to the needs of the AI/ML community.

The Docker universe is vast, dynamic, and ever-evolving. As we glimpse into the ongoing developments, we're reminded of Docker's commitment to innovation, its focus on the community, and its unwavering dedication to enhancing the software development and deployment world. The future, while unpredictable, promises exciting times ahead for Docker and the broader container community. As we steer through this technological epoch, Docker remains the lighthouse, guiding us through the intricate waters of containerization.

Emerging Trends

Docker has emerged as a pivotal player in shaping how applications are developed, packaged, and deployed in the rapidly evolving technology landscape. As containerization continues to gain traction, Docker finds itself at the intersection of various technological advancements, trends, and paradigms. It is paramount to explore the emerging trends in the Docker realm to understand its future trajectory and the broader implications for the software world. This deep dive into the unfolding trends will offer a quick look into what lies ahead for Docker, containerization, and the overarching software ecosystem.

One cannot discuss the future of Docker without mentioning the increasing adoption of microservices. Containerization concepts are ideally aligned with this architectural paradigm, which builds applications as a set of independently deployable, loosely connected services. Docker's lightweight, consistent, and isolated environment ensures that each microservice runs reliably, regardless of where it's deployed. As more organizations transition from monolithic to microservices architectures, Docker's role becomes increasingly pivotal. The trend suggests a future where applications are even more decentralized, and Docker, along with orchestration tools, becomes the backbone of such distributed systems.

Serverless computing, another buzzword in the tech space, refers to a cloud-computing model that can reduce complexity in deploying code into production. While serverless often revolves around functions-as-a-service (FaaS), there's a growing interest in leveraging containers in this model. Docker, given its nature, is perfectly suited for this. Emerging platforms are looking at ways to run Docker containers in a serverless environment, combining the best of both worlds. This integration promises a future where developers can deploy ephemeral, event-driven containers, and fully managed by cloud providers.

The ongoing data revolution has catalyzed the emergence of edge computing, where computation occurs closer to the data source, like IoT devices. Given the constraints at the edge – limited resources, intermittent connectivity, and varied environments – there's a need for lightweight, consistent, and portable solutions. Docker containers naturally fit this bill. The trend is moving towards using Docker in edge devices, ensuring applications run consistently in a centralized data center or on a remote device in the field.

With the rise in container adoption, security concerns have inevitably cropped up. Docker, being at the forefront of container technology, is actively involved in introducing and promoting better security standards. We're witnessing trends toward more secure container runtimes, improved isolation mechanisms, and comprehensive vulnerability scanning. There's a proactive shift towards making Docker and the container ecosystem as secure as possible, emphasizing secure image signing, runtime security, and tighter integration with enterprise security systems.

As applications become more complex and distributed, traditional monitoring tools fall short. There's a growing trend in enhancing observability in Dockerized environments. Advanced monitoring solutions are being developed to offer insights into the containers and the applications running within them. This holistic approach ensures that developers and operators can trace issues across the entire stack, from infrastructure to application logic.

Docker's versatility means it doesn't operate in a vacuum. There's a growing trend of integrating Docker with emerging technologies. Whether it's AI, machine learning, or blockchain, Docker is becoming the preferred environment for developing, testing, and deploying applications based on these technologies. Its consistency ensures that complex applications run seamlessly across different stages and platforms, often requiring specific dependencies and configurations.

Environmental concerns are pushing the tech world towards more sustainable practices. Due to its efficient utilization of resources compared to traditional virtualization methods, Docker is inherently more environmentally friendly. The trend suggests a future where Docker and containerization play a crucial role in green computing initiatives, minimizing waste of computational resources and, by extension, energy.

An undeniable trend in the Docker ecosystem is the relentless focus on improving the developer experience. Recognizing that developers are at the core of any technological innovation, Docker is continuously refining its toolset. From intuitive GUIs for container management to simplified clustering solutions and enhanced local development environments, Docker ensures that developers spend less time wrestling with infrastructure and more time coding.

Open source is at the heart of Docker, and the future sees even more collaboration and community involvement. Initiatives like the Moby Project underscore Docker's commitment to fostering a rich, collaborative ecosystem. The trend is clear: Docker is not just a tool but a community-driven platform, with contributions from developers worldwide shaping its future.

Artificial Intelligence (AI) and Machine Learning (ML) are revolutionizing industries, from healthcare to finance. These technologies require specific dependencies, large datasets, and specialized environments. Docker streamlines the process of setting up these environments. For instance, researchers can bundle their ML models, libraries, and dependencies into a Docker image, ensuring that the model runs consistently on a local machine or in a cloud-based production environment. Moreover, platforms like TensorFlow have released Docker images that help users set up their environments without the complexities traditionally associated with ML development.

Another groundbreaking technology where Docker is making strides is blockchain. Setting up blockchain nodes for Ethereum, Bitcoin, or other platforms can be a complex task. With Docker, however, developers can deploy nodes seamlessly, allowing for faster testing and development of blockchain applications. For instance, the Ethereum platform has official Docker images, which helps rapidly set up Ethereum nodes and test decentralized applications.

The Internet of Things (IoT) is a burgeoning field with devices ranging from smart thermostats to industrial sensors. These devices come with varied computational capacities and run in diverse environments. Docker's promise of "build once, run anywhere" is especially significant here. By containerizing IoT applications, developers ensure that the software behaves consistently across various devices. This consistency can prove crucial when IoT devices are deployed in remote or hard-to-access locations.

Docker's security has evolved over the years. Initially, there were concerns about Docker's isolation level, especially compared to traditional VMs. Today, however, Docker has mechanisms like user namespaces, seccomp profiles, and AppArmor integration, which enhance container isolation. Moreover, tools like Docker Bench for Security provide automated checks against best-practice security benchmarks. Docker's security-focused trajectory promises even tighter security measures in the future, with ongoing work in areas like secure image verification and runtime security enhancements.

Another emerging trend is Docker's growing adoption in the academic and research spheres. Given the need for reproducibility in research, Docker offers an ideal solution. Researchers can bundle their experiments, data, and tools into Docker containers, ensuring that peers can reproduce their results without wading through the challenges of setting up complex environments. This trend is particularly prominent in data-intensive fields like bioinformatics, where tools and dependencies can be especially intricate.

With organizations increasingly adopting multi-cloud strategies to avoid vendor lock-in and enhance availability, Docker's portability becomes even more valuable. A Docker container running on an AWS environment will run just as efficiently on Google Cloud or Azure. This trend of multi-cloud deployments, facilitated by Docker, will likely grow as organizations strive for enhanced resilience and flexibility.

Docker has played a crucial role in the democratization of DevOps. Previously, setting up, maintaining, and scaling applications required significant infrastructural knowledge. Today, Docker and orchestration tools like Kubernetes have simplified these processes.

Developers, without deep infrastructural expertise, can now deploy and scale applications. This trend leads to a more collaborative tech environment, where the barriers between developers and operations are increasingly blurred.

With its transformative potential, Docker continues to be at the helm of technological innovation. As we've delved deeper into the myriad ways Docker is shaping the tech landscape, it becomes evident that its impact transcends containerization. Docker is a testament to technology's potential to drive change, from facilitating groundbreaking research to democratizing DevOps. The highlighted trends offer a glimpse into Docker's future and the future of software development and deployment. As Docker continues to evolve, it's poised to remain at the forefront of the tech revolution, influencing practices, paradigms, and principles for years to come.

CONCLUSION

Docker CLI Reference Guide

Docker has become an essential tool in the modern software development landscape. Whether it's for containerizing applications, ensuring consistent environments across development and production, or streamlining the deployment process, Docker's significance can't be overstated. At the heart of interacting with Docker is its Command-Line Interface (CLI), which provides a comprehensive set of commands and options, allowing developers to manage every aspect of the Docker ecosystem. In this section, we'll delve into the depths of the Docker CLI, discussing its structure, key commands, and nuances.

Before we dive into the specifics of Docker commands, it's crucial to understand the general structure of the Docker CLI. The CLI has been designed to be intuitive, following a docker <command> <sub-command> <options> pattern. For instance, when managing containers, the primary command would be docker container, followed by sub-commands like create, start, or stop. Options further define the operation's specifics or modify its behavior.

Containers are Docker's primary building blocks, and the CLI provides a rich set of commands to manage them. Using docker container create, one can instantiate a new container, while docker container start and docker container stop allow starting and stopping containers, respectively. But Docker goes beyond just the basics. Commands like docker container pause can halt all processes within a container, and docker container unpause resumes them. This nuanced control is especially valuable in debugging or resource management scenarios.

For inspecting containers, docker container inspect offers detailed information about a container's configuration, state, and network settings. The returned JSON output provides an exhaustive look into the container, from its creation options to its current status.

Images, essentially snapshots of containers, are crucial for Docker's promise of consistency. The CLI offers a suite of commands for image management. One can fetch images from Docker Hub or other registries using docker image pull. Conversely, docker image push allows developers to push their custom images to registries, facilitating collaboration or deployment.

Creating custom images, often a critical part of the development workflow, involves a docker image build. This command uses Dockerfiles, which are scripts containing instructions for building images. The resulting images can be listed using docker image ls and detailed information about a specific image can be obtained using docker image inspect.

Docker's strength doesn't just lie in containerization but also in its networking capabilities. The CLI's networking commands let users manage the communication between containers. One can instantiate custom networks with docker network create, allowing specified containers to communicate. Similarly, docker network connect and docker network disconnect facilitate adding or removing containers from networks.

Data persistence, crucial for many applications, is managed in Docker using volumes. The CLI provides commands like docker volume create for initializing new volumes, docker volume ls for listing all available volumes, and docker volume inspect for obtaining detailed information about a specific volume.

Docker's CLI doesn't just cater to the basics but also provides advanced features that cater to sophisticated use cases. For instance, docker stack commands allow managing Docker stacks, a collection of services that can be deployed together. Docker Swarm, Docker's orchestration solution, can be managed using commands like docker swarm init, docker node ls, and docker service create.

Docker Compose, a tool for defining multi-container Docker applications, also has its own set of CLI commands, though they start with docker-compose instead of just docker.

While Docker's CLI is exhaustive, using it efficiently requires adherence to best practices. It's advisable to regularly clean up unused containers and images, using commands like docker container prune and docker image prune, respectively. This ensures optimal resource utilization.

Furthermore, while the CLI offers a lot of power, it's essential to use it judiciously. For instance, running containers with restricted permissions, using the --user option, enhances security. Regularly updating Docker and keeping abreast of changes to the CLI also ensures a smooth and secure experience.

The Docker CLI is a testament to Docker's philosophy of providing powerful features while ensuring usability. Whether you're a developer just starting with Docker or a seasoned DevOps professional, the CLI is the primary gateway to Docker's capabilities. From basic tasks like creating containers to advanced operations like managing Docker Swarm clusters, the CLI provides the tools necessary. As Docker continues to evolve, so will its CLI, further solidifying Docker's place in the modern software development and deployment ecosystem.

Summary

Software development has witnessed various technological advances that have revolutionized how developers approach, design, and deploy their applications. One such groundbreaking innovation is Docker. As we embarked on this extensive exploration of Docker, its concepts, applications, and nuances, we've delved into a plethora of subjects, each as crucial as the next in appreciating the full potential and scope of Docker. In this section, we aim to consolidate the knowledge shared, weaving together a holistic understanding of Docker and its place in the modern tech ecosystem.

At its core, Docker is a platform for developing, shipping, and running container applications. Born from the necessity to resolve the age-old dilemma of "it works on my machine," Docker provides a consistent application environment, from development to deployment. The inception of Docker was not just the birth of another tech tool; it represented a paradigm shift. Instead of provisioning and managing full-fledged virtual machines, Docker presented a lightweight, efficient, and swift solution by harnessing containerization.

Docker's magic lies in containers, which are isolated, lightweight execution environments. Unlike traditional virtualization, which requires running multiple OS instances, containers share the host's OS, making them more efficient and faster. This distinction also highlights the difference between containers and virtual machines, with the former being less resource-intensive and more adaptable.

Docker's architecture, consisting of the Docker Daemon, Client, and Images, enables its streamlined functionality. The Docker Daemon is the persistent procedure that manages Docker containers, while the Docker Client is the primary means through which many developers interact with Docker. On the other hand, Docker Images are lightweight, standalone, and executable software packages that encapsulate everything required to run a piece of software, ensuring consistency across platforms and environments.

Understanding the life cycle of containers and mastering commands such as docker run, pull, push, and build provides developers with granular control over their applications. Moreover, Docker facilitates detailed inspection and management of containers, offering insights and ensuring optimal performance.

A significant portion of Docker's prowess is its ability to create customized images tailored to developers' needs. Using Dockerfiles, developers can script the creation of images, ensuring precision and repeatability. Post creation, managing these images becomes paramount, and Docker provides a comprehensive suite of commands for this, from listing to inspecting images.

Docker's networking capabilities ensure that containers can communicate efficiently. With various network types such as Bridge, Host, Overlay, and None, Docker offers flexibility in network management, ensuring isolation or communication as required.

Data persistence, a fundamental requirement for many applications, is catered to by Docker's volume management. The use of bind mounts, tmpfs mounts, and the understanding of data persistence ensures that data is stored efficiently and portable across different Docker instances.

Docker isn't just about running singular containers; it's about orchestrating potentially hundreds or thousands of them in harmony. This orchestration is made possible with tools like Docker Compose, which allows for defining multi-container applications, and Docker Swarm, which is designed for clustering and scheduling Docker containers.

Docker's role in modern development practices such as Continuous Integration/Continuous Deployment (CI/CD) and microservices architecture showcases its adaptability and importance. Docker ensures that the CI/CD pipelines are consistent, and deployments are smooth. In microservices, Docker containers offer the perfect environment for these small, independent services, ensuring scalability, manageability, and resilience.

Docker's vast landscape also covers essential aspects like security, with best practices to ensure that containers are efficient and secure. Monitoring and logging tools integrated with Docker ensure that developers and administrators have a clear view of their applications' health and performance.

Additionally, Docker has facilitated the simplification of setting up development environments, ensuring that every developer, regardless of their platform or toolset, has a consistent and reliable environment to work in.

As with any technology, Docker is not static. The Docker ecosystem continually evolves, with new features, tools, and best practices emerging regularly. From the inception of Docker to the current day, the community and the industry have witnessed its transformative power. With ongoing developments and emerging trends, Docker is set to remain at the forefront of the containerization revolution, steering the tech world towards more efficient, consistent, and scalable solutions.

This summary encapsulates the journey through Docker's expansive realm. From its foundational concepts to its advanced applications, Docker stands as a testament to innovation in the tech world. Its impact on software development, deployment, and orchestration is profound, making it an indispensable tool in the modern developer's toolkit. As we look to the future, Docker's role in shaping and redefining the contours of tech solutions seems promising, ensuring that the software world remains dynamic, adaptable, and ever-evolving.

Call to Action

In a rapidly evolving technological landscape, adapting and staying ahead is not just desirable; it's imperative. Docker, a pioneering force in containerization, beckons developers, organizations, and the broader tech community to embrace its potential fully. This is not merely an endorsement of a tool or platform but a call to action, urging stakeholders to recognize and harness the transformative power of Docker. In this section, we aim to underscore the urgency, the rationale, and the roadmap to make the most of what Docker offers.

It's undeniable: the technological zeitgeist is characterized by swift change. With the demand for scalable, reliable, and quick-to-market applications, legacy systems and traditional development paradigms are increasingly proving to be bottlenecks. Every delay in updating infrastructure, every hiccup in deployment, and every inconsistency across environments translates to lost opportunities, diminished user trust, and tangible financial implications. Here, Docker presents itself as more than just a solution; it's a paradigm shift. And to not act upon its offerings is to risk obsolescence.

At the heart of Docker lies the principle of containerization, which, in essence, encapsulates an application with its environment. This means developers no longer hear the oft-repeated cry, "But it worked on my machine!" It's a promise of consistency, from a developer's workstation to a test environment, and then to production.

Imagine the power in the hands of a developer who can confidently state that if it works on their machine, it will work anywhere. This eradicates a class of bugs and deployment issues plaguing traditional development. But it's not just about bug reduction. It's about agility. Docker containers can be spun up in seconds, allowing for rapid testing and iteration. It's about efficiency. Gone are the days of provisioning heavy virtual machines that mimic production environments. Instead, lightweight containers that share the host's operating system can be used, consuming a fraction of the resources.

The call to action is clear, but how does one navigate the Docker landscape? Firstly, it's essential to grasp the foundational concepts, such as images and containers, their differences, and their lifecycle. One must then venture into more advanced territories, understanding networking, data persistence, and the orchestration of multi-container applications.

Security, often a concern when adopting new technologies, is an integral part of the Docker ecosystem. Following best practices is crucial, ensuring that containers are efficient and secure. Monitoring, logging, and performance optimization should be part and parcel of any Docker strategy, ensuring applications are not only functional but also robust and performant.

While individuals stand to benefit immensely from Docker, the true potential is unlocked when entire organizations realign their strategies around Docker and containerization. Continuous Integration and Continuous Deployment pipelines become more streamlined, ensuring that software releases are faster and more consistent. Microservices, a trend that has proven to be more than just a passing fad, finds a natural ally in Docker, with each service encapsulated in its container, ensuring scalability and manageability.

Docker, while powerful, is not isolated. It's part of a broader ecosystem, and its success can be attributed, in part, to a vibrant community of developers, sysadmins, and organizations. There's a shared wealth of Dockerfiles, images, and best practices, making it easier for newcomers to get on board. This call to action is also a plea for collaboration. By sharing knowledge, tools, and solutions, the tech community can ensure that Docker's potential is not just realized but amplified.

Embracing Docker is not about discarding what one knows or starting afresh. It's about augmentation. Traditional skills in software development, systems administration, and architecture are all enhanced when viewed through the Docker lens. It's a call to be future-ready, adaptable, and at the forefront of technological innovation.

In this ever-evolving tech landscape, Docker emerges as another tool in the developer's arsenal and a transformative force. Therefore, this call to action is not just about using Docker; it's about reimagining the way we approach software development and deployment. It's a call to be part of a revolution, to shape the future of tech, and to ensure that as developers, sysadmins, and organizations, we are not just participants in this tech narrative but pioneers leading the charge. So, as we stand at this juncture, the question is not whether we should embrace Docker, but how swiftly and wholeheartedly we can do so.

What to look out for in the future

The world of technology, especially that of software development and deployment, is in a state of perpetual flux. With the rise of containerization and its profound implications on how we handle applications, Docker, as a pioneering force in this domain, has secured its position at the forefront. However, like all technological marvels, Docker too will not remain static. Several transformative shifts, expansions, and challenges in the Docker landscape become evident as we look ahead. This section seeks to journey into the foreseeable future of Docker, highlighting what stakeholders can expect, prepare for, and capitalize on.

Rising Adoption across Industries

While Docker's impact on the technology sector has been palpable, we anticipate its tentacles will reach deeper into industries that have traditionally been slower to adapt to newer tech solutions. From healthcare to finance, from retail to manufacturing, Docker's proposition of consistency across different environments presents an attractive proposition. Docker's prominence will only grow as more sectors recognize the value of rapid application development and deployment.

Integration with Emerging Technologies

With advancements in the Internet of Things (IoT), Artificial Intelligence (AI), and Machine Learning (ML), there's a palpable need for infrastructural solutions that can handle the complex, voluminous, and often real-time demands these technologies place on systems. Docker's containerized approach could be a game-changer here. Imagine edge devices in IoT networks swiftly deploying containerized applications, or AI models being consistently tested and deployed across varied environments using Docker. The symbiosis between Docker and these burgeoning technologies can potentially rewrite the rulebook of development and deployment.

Diversification of Orchestration Solutions
While Kubernetes has emerged as the dominant force in container orchestration, working seamlessly with Docker, the future might witness the rise of more orchestration solutions, each catering to nuanced needs. The community will likely develop these to simplify, enhance, or specialize container management, responding to specific industry demands or challenges that might arise with increased Docker adoption.

Enhancements in Security
With the rise in cyber threats and the unique challenges Docker and containerization might present, there's an impending evolution in how Docker handles security. Future iterations of Docker will likely have more built-in security features, from enhanced image scanning to more secure networking configurations. Additionally, as Docker containers become more prevalent, a parallel ecosystem of security tools and best practices explicitly catering to containerized applications will emerge.

Focus on Sustainability and Efficiency

As the world grapples with the challenges of sustainability, there will be increased scrutiny on the energy consumption patterns of digital infrastructureGivenven its potential for lightweight and efficient deployme Dockernt, might become a centerpiece in discussions around green computing. Future Docker versions and related tools could have features that allow monitoring and optimization of energy consumption, making containerization not just a choice for efficiency but also for environmental responsibility.

Education and Training

The increasing reliance on Docker will necessitate comprehensive education and training programs. As organizations across sectors adopt Docker, there will be a surging demand for professionals adept at harnessing its potential. This will spur educational institutions, online platforms, and even Docker's own community to create exhaustive training materials, courses, and certifications. For professionals in the tech domain, Docker expertise will soon transition from being a 'good-to-have' to a 'must-have.'

Community-driven Evolution

One of Docker's greatest strengths has been its vibrant community. As we look to the future, this community will play an even more crucial role. Whether it's developing plugins, identifying and rectifying vulnerabilities, or creating innovative solutions to unanticipated challenges, the community will be at the heart of Docker's evolution. Future Docker conventions and meet-ups will likely become hotbeds of innovation, where ideas are exchanged, solutions are brainstormed, and the course for Docker's journey is charted out.

Challenges in Standardization

As Docker and containerization become ubiquitous, there will be inevitable discussions on standardization. Different container tools, varied orchestration solutions, and many plugins can lead to fragmentation. The tech world will grapple with the challenge of ensuring that while innovation is not stifled, there's a certain standard that all Docker-related solutions adhere to. This will ensure interoperability, security, and consistency across the board.

In conclusion, one thing is clear in wrapping up this foray into Docker's future: Docker's journey is just beginning. The shifts we anticipate are incremental changes and potential revolutions in how we perceive application development and deployment. With its promise of containerization, Docker stands at the cusp of these changes, leading the charge. For developers, organizations, and anyone invested in the tech landscape, keeping an eye on Docker's trajectory is not just recommended; it's imperative. Embracing, adapting to, and contributing to Docker's evolution will be the hallmark of tech-savvy stakeholders in the times to come.

*Thank you for buying and reading/listening to our book.
If you found this book useful/helpful please take a few minutes
and leave a review on the platform where you purchased our book.
Your feedback matters greatly to us.*

www.ingramcontent.com/pod-product-compliance
Lightning Source LLC
LaVergne TN
LVHW021827060526
838201LV00058B/3549